Wild at Heart

'*Wild at Heart*' is a growing business selling a range of award-winning, artisan-made jellies, relishes and fruit cheeses, inspired by wild, native or ancient fruits and based on traditional English recipes. It was set up by Ginny Knox and Caro Willson. At school together they had shared many happy, sun-soaked days roaming the nearby fields and hedgerows, collecting crab apples and brambles to make into cakes, jellies and other delicious things. They both feel passionate about wild food, which is by definition local, seasonal, fresh and low in food miles. Not only this, but foods which grow in proximity on the same land are more likely to complement each other. Most importantly, gathering and cooking these foods is fabulous fun and directly connects us to our cultural heritage and helps bind us together as a community.

www.wildatheartfoods.co.uk

THE
HEDGEROW
COOKBOOK

By *Wild at Heart*

PAVILION

First published in 2013 by Pavilion Books

An imprint of Anova Books
10 Southcombe Street
London W14 ORA
www.anovabooks.com

ISBN: 978-1-86205-9566

10 9 8 7 6 5 4 3 2 1

A CIP record for this book is available from the British Library

Commissioning editor: Fiona Holman
Art director: Georgina Hewitt
Photographer: Cristian Barnett
Designer: Allan Somerville
Copy editor: Maggie Ramsay

Reproduction by Mission, Hong Kong
Printed by 1010 Printing International Ltd, China

Contents

Introduction

The inspiration for our company, Wild at Heart, came from our kitchen windows: Caro's gazing at Kentish orchards with their neat rows of cultivated apple trees, punctuated by bright red or yellow crab apples, and Ginny's overlooking the commons of Surrey, fringed with hedges of damson and sloe.

We have been friends more or less for ever, with a shared and abiding passion for food: making it, reading about it, talking about it and eating lots of it. As children we scoured the hedgerows of Sussex with our mothers, braving nettles and thorns for the prize of a sweet, juicy blackberry crumble. And our delight in foraging has grown over the years. We each have cupboards bursting with little pots of rich purple damson cheese and jewel-like crab apple jelly, bottles of dark, fruity sloe gin and heady elderflower cordial. Cupboards we can't resist peeking at on grey winter days, to raise a smile and make our hearts swell.

Having slaved at our careers in very large finance and food companies respectively for well over 20 years, we realized we were both yearning for a change of pace and direction. We decided to 'do something' together and it was obvious that the something would hark back to our shared foodie roots.

So, we set out to rediscover the pleasures of wild, native or ancient fruits that had perhaps been overlooked in this supermarket age of perfect strawberries all year round and hang the air miles. The laying down of bottles and jars during the autumn to sustain us until spring is one of the most deeply satisfying things a cook can do. A whiff of homemade raspberry jam instantly conjures up an early summer's day, a tangy pot of chutney celebrates the abundance of harvest time and transforms a sad wedge of cheddar cheese into a glorious lunch.

We have been inspired by nature's bounty but not bound by it. The discovery of an ancient quince or medlar tree in a long-neglected kitchen garden is as much cause for celebration as a basketful of berries collected during a country walk. Indeed the line between wild and cultivated is often pretty thin and we haven't felt the need for a strict 'wild-only' straitjacket, preferring instead to call our freely gathered ingredients 'wild, native, ancient or otherwise unfashionable'.

We also wanted to make food that would taste homemade because it was wholesome and true. A preparation of mint, crab apples, vinegar and sugar – or one made with water, colouring, gelling agent and mint oil? Both are called mint jelly, but which would you rather have on your plate, which would you make at home? This is the ethos of the foods we sell and it underpins the recipes in this book.

And so, in March 2011, having spent an autumn picking fruit until we could barely move and a winter boiling away like witches at their cauldrons, we started selling our traditional accompaniments for meats and cheeses under the name Wild at Heart: fruity crab apple and medlar jellies, little pots of damson and quince cheeses, rich wild plum chutney and mellow red onion marmalade. We were completely blown away by the response from our customers, the press and serious food experts. It was an amazing first year. Our absolutely best moments, though, were when someone tasted, say, our crab apple jelly, and was delightedly transported back to their childhood and, almost invariably, something their mother or grandmother used to make.

We gradually built up a loyal customer base through local farm shops, delis and butchers. In our second year we were able to secure larger supplies of our rare, fruity raw materials directly from local farmers

are masses of edible wild plants and fruits that we have not included because they are hard to find, hard to identify or just don't taste very nice! We firmly believe that foraging should be a pleasure, one that connects us to the very specific area in which we live, what grows there, what tastes good there. Food for free is wonderful as long as it also delivers on taste: we are not interested in hair shirts and we don't believe you will be, either.

However, we have discovered that deciding what to leave out of a book is much trickier than deciding what to put in it. Inevitably one book can't cover every delicious food you could forage, let alone the ones that we feel are overrated, such as wild sorrel (definitely not a patch on its cultivated version). We have also found ourselves reluctantly leaving out whole types of food such as roots (legality of gathering quite dubious), mushrooms (need their own book, as misidentification can have such serious consequences) and seaweeds (a bit impracticable for most people who don't live by the sea). And that's before we even started trying to whittle down our recipe list to the hundred or so we have had space to include!

Gathering food with friends or family, bringing it home and making something fabulous to eat has to be one of life's most ancient and pleasurable rituals. It connects us with our culture, our land and our history. It reminds us of what food should be: natural, local and fresh. In the UK, many of us have lost touch with the land to a far greater extent than our neighbours in continental Europe, where the calendar is often still marked with the traditional dates to gather nuts or a particular fruit. Many of us have picked blackberries at some point in our lives, but how many have gone beyond that and tried a wild leaf salad or a homemade damson fool?

This is a recipe book first and foremost, and we hope that you will be encouraged to take a walk and see what you can find growing near where you live, whether in the town or the countryside, and that you will be inspired to come home and cook up a real treat to share with your nearest and dearest.

Caro Willson and Ginny Knox
April 2013

and nurserymen, and Wild at Heart secured its first multiple listing. We are now excitedly making plans for new products and new distribution and looking forward to meeting more wonderfully dedicated food enthusiasts on the way!

The discovery of an ancient quince or medlar tree in a long-neglected kitchen garden is as much cause for celebration as a basketful of berries collected during a country walk

From there it was a very short step to the idea of a book that would celebrate many of the wonderful things that can be made by scouring the hedgerows, the woods and the lanes. Preserves, of course, but also drinks, savoury dishes, puddings, cakes, sweets and treats. Recipes to enjoy in season and stores to lay down for the leaner months. Above all, food that tastes utterly delicious. This is very important: there

A little on the law and common sense

You should not feel unduly worried about foraging, provided you apply some common sense to the rather unsatisfactory and sometimes almost contradictory laws prevailing.

You need permission to go onto land you do not own, in order to avoid trespassing (this does not apply in Scotland). This permission is implicit in, for example, National Trust and Forestry Commission land and other places such as nature reserves.

You have a common-law right to collect fruit, flowers, fungi and foliage as long as you are picking for your personal use and provided that what you are picking has not been planted as a crop. But you may not uproot a plant without the landowner's permission. This means that even if you are trespassing, you are not stealing and will not therefore face criminal prosecution. If the landowner is unhappy with your actions, he will have to sue you for damages in the civil courts (though we could not recommend testing this out!). You should, however, keep your eyes peeled for notices of any byelaw that overrides the above.

Care is needed on Sites of Special Scientific Interest (SSSIs), as it is technically illegal to pick any plant on them. Furthermore, land made newly accessible under the Countryside and Rights of Way Act 2000 (CROW) does not come with foraging rights unless these existed before the land was registered under the act.

Finally, some rare plants (not cited in this book) are protected by law and it obviously makes sense to be careful where you tread and what you are treading on and to pick a little here and there rather than stripping one area bare.

> ### Readers' notes
> 1 teaspoon = 5 ml;
> 1 tablespoon = 15ml.
>
> *All spoon measurements are level.*

Preserving: the basics

Traditional preserves: jam, jelly, chutney, cheese, butter

Traditional preserves can be kept unopened in a cool, dry place for up to 2 years, as long as they are stored in sterilized jars. Once opened, keep in the fridge and, in general, aim to eat within 4–8 weeks. But use your common sense. If it looks or smells off, it probably is, and we advise throwing it away!

You will need clean glass jars, which we recommend you seal with metal screw-top lids with a plasticized lining – not the plastic lids from instant coffee or peanut butter jars. It is fine to recycle jars, but do check that they are completely undamaged before using them again. Lids can also be re-used as long as the plasticized lining is intact. Screw-top lids are by far the most straightforward option, and are in any case essential for vinegar-based preserves to prevent corrosion. You *can* use wax discs with a cellophane and elastic band cover, but frankly why would you? There is no tangible advantage and you will find it is very fiddly and a nightmare once the preserve is in use.

You have a common law right to collect wild fruit, flowers, fungi and foliage as long as you are picking for your personal use

We have deliberately been quite vague when describing how much preserve you can expect to make from any given recipe. That's partly because preserving, especially with wild foods, is as much alchemy as science: among other unquantifiables, fruit varies in water content, pectin and the amount of wastage from pips and skins. We also know you're going to be using different sized jars; when we say a 'large jar' we mean a standard jam jar, around 310–450 g/11 oz–1 lb. A 'small jar' is even more subjective, but is often practical if you don't want to eat all your precious jam or jelly at once – and also looks pretty as a gift or added to a hamper. When it comes to sterilizing your jars, it's a good idea to bung a couple

of extra jars and lids in to sterilize as a matter of course; that way any variance in jar size shouldn't matter.

Sterilization

Before using your jars and lids, they will need to be sterilized. There are three ways of doing this: the easiest way is to place them in the oven at 100°C/212°F/less than gas mark ¼ for 30 minutes. If you prefer, you can put them through the dishwasher on a hot cycle. You can also immerse the jars in a saucepan of water, bring it to the boil, then boil rapidly for 10 minutes; briefly scald the lids in boiling water. In each of the last two cases the jars and lids need to be dried before use. Place them upside down on a clean, thick tea towel and leave until they are thoroughly dry.

Once the jars have been sterilized, they should be used straight away (or as soon as they are dry if using a wet sterilization method). Using a jam funnel, ladle or spoon the hot preserve into the warm jars and fill to within 5 mm/¼ in of the top. Seal immediately and label when cold.

Useful equipment
- large saucepan or preserving pan
- wooden spoon for stirring, large spoon for skimming
- jam funnel
- jam thermometer (optional)
- jelly bag – or improvise with a sieve or colander lined with muslin (cheesecloth)
- jars/bottles and lids – and labels
- food mill with fine, medium and coarse discs for puréeing all kinds of fruit at the same time as removing the stones/pips and much of the skin. The alternative – rubbing the fruit through a fine sieve – is unbelievably hard work

Testing for setting point/readiness

Before filling your sterilized jars, you need to test that the preserve is ready. In the case of jams and jellies, this means that it needs to reach setting point. A good set depends on the presence of pectin (found within the fruit cell walls and in the pips and stones), acid and sugar in the correct proportions. Apples and gooseberries are high in pectin, while other fruits won't set well unless you adjust the acidity (for example by adding lemon juice) or add extra pectin (you can buy jam sugar, with added pectin). We've suggested the best way to get a good set in individual recipes.

To test the set of jams and jellies, our preferred method is the wrinkle test: place a clean plate in the fridge and, when you think your potion is ready, spoon a blob onto the plate and return to the fridge for a couple of minutes. If setting point has been reached, a skin will form on the top and it will wrinkle when you push it with your finger (see photograph page 9). If not, keep the jam boiling for an additional 5 minutes, then try again. You can use a jam thermometer to show when you have reached the technical setting point of 104.5°C/220°F, but in our experience this can be a little unreliable. We find the jam thermometer is most useful as a guide to when to start wrinkle testing.

Chutneys are ready when their liquid has thickened so that if you scrape a wooden spoon across the pan you can see the bottom of the pan for a split second or two. You can also test by spooning some onto a plate and if the liquid stays around the mound, it is ready. If it runs across the plate, keep boiling for an additional 5 minutes.

Fruit cheeses are ready when they will stay in a mound on a plate with no liquid running off. Fruit butters will be fine as soon as they start thickening in the pan: they should be easily spreadable.

Bottling: cordial, syrup, wine, vodka, vinegar, pickled fruit or nuts, fruit in alcohol

Bottled drinks and fruits can be kept for months, or even years, as long as you store them in clean glass bottles with well-fitting screw-top or swing-top lids, which should be sterilized in the same way as the jam jars above. You can buy lovely bottles from specialist suppliers, and recycling is also a good option as long as the bottles are in perfect condition. Don't forget to use vinegar-proof lids when appropriate.

Homemade wines and beers do require some basic equipment that you are very unlikely to have in the house, but a visit to a home-brewing supplier or their website should soon demystify the world of demijohns and airlocks. The great thing is to experiment! To sterilize the tubs and tubes, you can buy Campden tablets from home-brew suppliers, or Milton sterilizing fluid or tablets from pharmacies.

Water bath sterilization
If you want to extend the shelf life of fruit cordials and syrups to a year or more, you will need to sterilize the bottles once they have been filled and sealed. Fill the bottles to within 3.5 cm/1¼ inches of the tops to allow for expansion. Swing tops should be fully sealed, screw tops should be closed lightly and then fully tightened once they have been sterilized. Place a trivet or folded tea towel in the bottom of a saucepan deep enough to submerge the bottles fully: this will prevent them from cracking. Stand the bottles in the pan and cover them with warm water. Gradually bring the water to simmering point (88°C/190°F) and maintain this for 20 minutes. Turn off the heat and allow the bottles to stand in the water for 5 minutes. Remove the bottles from the saucepan (scoop some of the water out first to avoid burning yourself!) and tighten any screw tops fully.

Seasonal Availability

	JAN	FEB	MAR	APR	MAY	JUN	JUL	AUG	SEP	OCT	NOV	DEC
Bilberries								●	●			
Blackberries								●	●	●		
Chestnuts										●	●	
Crab Apples								●	●	●		
Dandelions			●	●	●							
Damsons								●	●			
Elderflowers					●	●						
Elderberries								●	●	●		
Hazelnuts								●	●	●		
Marsh Samphire						●	●	●	●			
Medlars										●	●	●
Nettles			●	●	●							
Quinces									●	●	●	
Rowan Berries							●	●	●	●		
Sloes									●	●	●	●
Walnuts									●	●		
Wild Cherries						●	●					
Wild Garlic			●	●	●	●						
Wild Plums							●	●	●			
Wild Raspberries							●	●	●			
Wild Rose Flowers					●	●	●					
Wild Rose Hips								●	●	●	●	
Wild Sorrel			●	●	●		●	●	●			
Wild Strawberries							●	●	●			

Flowers & Hips

Wild flowers and blossom clothe our countryside in yellow, blue, pink and white and very often herald the delicious harvest of fruit to come. In harsher times flowers were used for their medicinal qualities, or simply as part of the patchwork of wild and cultivated foods that added variety to the diets of rich and poor alike.

These days, wild flowers such as primroses and borage are often strewn on salads in fashionable restaurants and our focus is more on the visual appeal than the nutritional benefit of such ingredients. They do indeed work wonderfully as eye candy, but we feel that it is worth having a few recipes up your sleeve to showcase the full loveliness of a few of the easiest wild flowers to find and use. The flavour and scent of a handful of flowers collected during a walk can be captured in an incomparable drink or preserve. Later in the year, once the wild roses have started to fade, the hips take over, providing wild interest almost up to Christmas.

The image shows elderflowers.

Elderflowers

Hedgerows everywhere south of Dundee are a riot of frothy, creamy elderflowers in May and June. There are one or two other plants that may be mistaken for elderflowers at a glance, but one sniff will soon sort out any confusion. The aroma is unmistakable, full of heady perfume, sometimes reminiscent of bananas and sometimes sour, likened by some to cat's wee.

There is a lot of superstition associated with elder trees, which have been thought to have magical qualities. It is said that the wood should never be brought into the house and burned because it will release the devil in it. Some say that Judas hanged himself from an elder tree and that the cross of Christ was made from its wood. More optimistically, it is meant to protect the household from evil if planted nearby and is apparently never struck by lightning.

The flowers are tiny with yellow stamens and form large flat plate-like sprays on a strong stalk. In earlier times, children would push out the soft centre of young stems and make simple whistles or pop guns. Traditionally elderflowers were infused into cordials, vinegars and wines to impart their amazing muscat flavour. Elderflower vinegar is indeed a wonderful seasoning for fish. To make it, simply infuse some elderflower heads in cider vinegar for 4–5 days, then strain into sterilized bottles.

Cut the whole heads, with a short length of the stalk, as soon as the dew has dried and handle them gently: they are as delicate as they look. Don't wash them, just shake them gently to remove any insects. If you can't use them on the same day, the heads *can* be frozen or dried, but why would you want to miss out on the fragrant loveliness of fresh elderflowers?

Elderflower Cordial

Elderflower cordial makes the most wonderful drink when diluted with water or sparkling wine, and is also a superb storecupboard ingredient to add a fragrant twist to all sorts of yummy cakes and puddings; we've included some examples in this chapter.

The cordial can be frozen, either in plastic bottles (remember to leave a little space for expansion) or in ice cube trays, which are handy if you need only a small quantity. Store in the freezer for up to 3 months. The frozen cordial will remain slightly soft and sticky because of the high sugar content, so make sure you use flexible ice cube trays to make unmoulding easier.

35 elderflower heads
3 unwaxed lemons
1.3 kg/3 lb/6½ cups
   granulated sugar
55 g/2 oz citric acid

Makes about 2 litres/3½ pints/ 2 quarts

1 Gently shake the elderflower heads to remove any insects and place in a large bowl. Pare off the lemon zest in large strips, using a knife or potato peeler, and add to the elderflowers. Slice the lemons thickly and add those too. Put the sugar and 1.4 litres/2½ pints/scant 6 cups water in a saucepan over a medium heat and stir until the sugar has dissolved completely. Then pour the sugar solution over the elderflower mixture, add the citric acid and stir thoroughly. Cover with a clean cloth and leave at room temperature for 24–48 hours.

2 The next day, strain the cordial through a sieve lined with muslin (cheesecloth) or a jelly bag. Either freeze as described above or pour into sterilized glass bottles and seal. The cordial will keep for 2–3 weeks in a cool, dark place. If you would like to keep it for up to a year, follow the water bath sterilization method (see page 11).

Elderflower Champagne

Every year we look forward to the elderflower season: it heralds the beginning of summer and only a short wait until this delicious drink will be ready to guzzle in the sun. It is very pretty, fragrant and not overly alcoholic. Best of all, it is easy and requires no special equipment to make.

650 g/1 lb 7 oz/3¼ cups
  granulated sugar
1 lemon
6 elderflower heads
2 tbsp white wine vinegar

Makes about
4.5 litres/
1 gallon/
4½ quarts

1 Put the sugar in a saucepan with 1 litre/1¾ pints/4 cups cold water and heat gently, stirring occasionally, until the sugar has dissolved completely. Leave to cool.

2 Pare off the lemon zest in large strips and place these, as well as the lemon juice, into your largest china bowl or a food-grade plastic bucket. Add the elderflower heads, the vinegar and an additional 3.5 litres/6 pints/3½ quarts cold water, then add the cooled sugar syrup and stir gently. Cover with a clean cloth and leave to steep. The champagne should start to ferment (you will notice small bubbles) after about 2 days, although it may take slightly longer. Leave it to continue fermenting for another four days and then strain and bottle. Fill the bottles to about 2.5 cm/1 inch from the tops to allow for expansion and put them in a cool place to mature.

3 Elderflower champagne can explode in the bottle and it will make a sticky mess if it does, to say nothing of sending shards of glass everywhere. We recommend using strong plastic bottles with screw-top lids to avoid this problem. You can either recycle cola or lemonade bottles or buy new ones from home-brewing suppliers. It is wise to check them every few days and if the bottles seem to be expanding slightly around the middle, just loosen the lid very gently to release the excess fizz and then tighten the lid again.

4 You can drink the champagne after a couple of weeks, but it improves if left for two months or more. Caro once made such a vast amount that she was able to experiment with leaving it for almost a year and it was absolutely fine.

Grown-Up Elderflower Jelly

Jelly is an underrated pudding in our opinion, and it has so much to recommend it: it can be made a day or even two in advance, it looks gorgeous and the addition of Prosecco gives it a celebratory fizz. We served this on New Year's Eve and it totally hit the spot.

5 leaves of gelatine
300 ml/10 fl oz/1½ cups elderflower cordial (see page 15)
400 ml/14 fl oz/scant 1¾ cups Prosecco or other sparkling wine
About 125 g/4½ oz raspberries

1 Soak the gelatine in cold water for 5 minutes to soften. Put the elderflower cordial into a saucepan over a medium heat and bring to the boil; remove from the heat. Squeeze out the water from the gelatine leaves one by one and whisk them into the cordial. Once the gelatine has completely dissolved, add the Prosecco.

2 Place 3 or 4 raspberries in each of six champagne flutes or wine glasses, pour the jelly mixture gently over the fruit and put the glasses in the fridge for 6 hours or overnight, until set.

Makes 12 cakes

Elderflower Fairy Cakes

These little elderflower cakes are a delightful and delicate teatime treat. An English antidote to the craze for cupcakes weighed down under a mountain of buttercream!

Cakes:
125 g/4½ oz/1 cup self-raising flour
1 tsp baking powder
125 g/4½ oz/generous ½ cup butter, softened
125 g/4½ oz generous ½ cup caster (superfine) sugar
2 large eggs
7 tbsp elderflower cordial (see page 15)

To Decorate:
100 g/3½ oz/¾ cup icing (confectioners') sugar
2 tbsp elderflower cordial (see page 15)
12 sugar flowers (optional)

1 Preheat the oven to 180°C/350°F/gas mark 4 and line a 12-hole muffin tin with paper cases: silver ones will be most beautiful.

2 Stir the flour and baking powder together and set aside. Using an electric mixer, cream the butter and sugar together until they are pale and fluffy. Then add the eggs, one at a time, alternating with a spoonful of the flour mixture and whisking thoroughly after each addition. Finally stir in the remaining flour mixture and the elderflower cordial. Divide the cake mixture among the 12 paper cases. Bake for 15–20 minutes until the cakes are golden and spring back when pressed lightly. Leave to cool in the tin for 5 minutes and then turn out onto a wire rack and leave until completely cool.

3 To decorate, put the icing sugar in a bowl, add the elderflower cordial and stir thoroughly to make a thick paste. Gently spread the icing over the cakes, using a knife or the back of a spoon; dip the knife or spoon into a cup of very hot water after each cake. You can add a flower to the middle of each cake if you like.

Elderflower Sorbet

Homemade sorbets and ice creams beat anything you can buy in the shops hands down. This delicate sorbet is fabulous paired with a simple berry fruit salad and decorated with a sprig of mint (see photograph page 97).

150 g/5½ oz/¾ cup granulated sugar
1 lemon
8 tbsp elderflower cordial (see page 15)
1 egg white, lightly beaten

Serves 6

1 Put the sugar in a saucepan, add 150 ml/5 fl oz/²⁄₃ cup water and heat gently, stirring occasionally, until the sugar has completely dissolved. Pare off the lemon zest in strips, add to the sugar syrup and remove from the heat. Leave to infuse for 30 minutes.

2 Meanwhile, squeeze the lemon juice and dilute the elderflower cordial with 200 ml/7 fl oz/generous ¾ cup water. Strain the sugar syrup into a bowl, stir in the lemon juice and the diluted cordial and then incorporate the egg white, stirring as little as possible. Pour it into an ice-cream maker and churn according to the manufacturer's instructions. Alternatively, to freeze without using an ice-cream maker, pour the mixture into a container and freeze, stirring briefly with a fork every 30 minutes to break up the ice crystals, until set.

3 The sorbet will keep in a covered container in the freezer for up to 2 months.

Elderflower & Gooseberry Jam

This jam combines two of the most distinctive and delicious flavours to be found in spring – nectar indeed! Gooseberries have high levels of acid and pectin, so the jam will set easily. It is relatively tart and is fabulous matched with cream, for example on scones or in an early-summer Victoria sponge. Perhaps served with a glass of elderflower champagne?

1.5 kg/3 lb 5 oz gooseberries
30 large elderflower heads
1.5 kg/3 lb 5 oz/7½ cups granulated sugar

Makes 6–7 large jars

1 Top, tail and wash the gooseberries and put them in a large saucepan or preserving pan with 200 ml/7 fl oz/generous ¾ cup cold water. Gently shake the elderflower heads to remove any insects, then strip the flowers from the stalks using a fork and add them to the pan. Simmer gently until the gooseberries are soft but still retain their shape.

2 Add the sugar and stir until it has dissolved completely. Increase the heat and boil rapidly until setting point is reached (see page 10). Remove from the heat and leave the jam to stand for 10 minutes. Stir and then spoon into warm, sterilized jars and seal immediately.

Elderflower Fritters

This is like a Japanese tempura: the ethereal batter compliments the frothy elderflowers beautifully. A light dusting of caster (superfine) sugar and a squeeze of lemon juice will suffice as accompaniments, but if you have more time, any concoction of cream, sugar and gooseberries could only enhance the loveliness.

12 large elderflower heads
Vegetable oil for deep-frying
85 g/3 oz/scant ¾ cup plain (all-purpose) flour
1 tbsp cornflour (cornstarch)
Pinch of baking powder
200 ml/7 fl oz/generous ¾ cup ice-cold sparkling water

1 Gently shake the elderflower heads to remove any insects. Put some paper towels on a plate, ready to drain the fritters. Heat the oil to 180°C/350°F, or until a cube of bread browns in 30 seconds.

2 Make the batter by mixing together the flour, cornflour and baking powder and then whisking the water in as quickly as possible. Don't overwhisk. Once the oil is very (scarily) hot, lower each elderflower head into the batter and deep-fry until it spreads out, at which point the batter will have cooked and started to darken. Remove from the pan and drain on the paper towel. Repeat with the remaining elderflower heads. Serve hot, sprinkled with sugar.

Elderflower Custard Tart

This is an elegant tart, with crisp, buttery pastry and a creamy/fruity, scented middle. An English answer to Tarte au Citron. Sometimes we are moved to sprinkle in a handful of fresh gooseberries with the custard, which is also really good. You could serve it with a few strawberries if you like, but we think it's best just on its own.

Pastry:
115 g/4 oz/scant 1 cup plain (all-purpose) flour
30 g/1 oz/2 tbsp caster (superfine) sugar
75 g/2¾ oz/5 tbsp cold butter
1 egg, separated

Custard:
2 eggs, plus 2 egg yolks
1 tbsp caster (superfine) sugar
300 ml/10 fl oz/1¼ cups double (heavy) cream
300 ml/10 fl oz/1¼ cups elderflower cordial (see page 15)
Icing (confectioners') sugar, for dusting

1 To make the pastry, whizz the flour, sugar and cold butter in a food processor until they resemble fine breadcrumbs. Add the egg yolk (reserve the white) and ½ tablespoon ice-cold water. Add a little extra water if necessary to bind the dough, but add it in tiny amounts. As soon as the dough begins to come together, remove it from the food processor, shape it into a disc, wrap in clingfilm (plastic wrap) and put it in the fridge for 20 minutes.

2 You will need a 22 cm/8½ inch diameter loose-bottomed tart tin. (It's harder to get this pastry right in a ceramic dish.) When the pastry is cool, but not totally fridge-cold and hard, roll it out until it is large enough to line the bottom and sides of the tin. We recommend leaving a little overhang when you trim the pastry, to allow for shrinkage in the oven: it won't be quite so perfect-looking but is much less risky with the custard filling. Prick the pastry all over with a fork. If you are using a tin, put it in the freezer for 20 minutes. If you are using a ceramic dish, put it into the fridge for 20–30 minutes. Preheat the oven to 180°C/350°F/gas mark 4. If the pastry is frozen or well chilled you should not have to fiddle about with lining it before baking.

3 Bake the pastry for 15 minutes. Remove from the oven and brush the bottom and sides of the pastry with the reserved egg white, then pop it back into the oven for 5 minutes. This will help to seal the pastry. Remove the pastry shell from the oven and reduce the oven temperature to 160°C/325°F/gas mark 3.

4 To make the custard, put the eggs, egg yolks, sugar, cream and elderflower cordial in a bowl and whisk them together thoroughly. Put the pastry shell on a large baking sheet in the oven, and pull the oven shelf out a bit. Pour the custard carefully into the pastry shell. Don't overfill it, as the pastry will turn to soggy mush if the custard overflows. Bake for about 35 minutes, but check it regularly after about 20 minutes. The custard should rise up slightly at the edges and be just set in the middle. Don't let it rise fully or the custard will split, which will spoil its looks and the texture won't be so good.

5 Remove the tart from the oven and leave it to cool completely. Don't worry if the surface cracks a bit. This is normal, as you can see from the picture opposite! Just before serving, dust with a little icing (confectioners') sugar.

Dandelions

The bright yellow flowers of the dandelion are common everywhere from early spring. Many health claims are made for dandelions, from the diuretic effect of the leaves (hence the French common name of pissenlit) to the antioxidant properties of the flowers. All parts of the dandelion are edible, though not always appetizing: the roots and older leaves can be bitter. We have fine-tuned a good recipe for the leaves (see page 58) and here offer you the two best uses of the flowers.

Dandelion Flower Wine

1 litre/about 2 pints/4 cups
  dandelion flowers
2 litres/3½ pints/2 quarts
  boiling water
4 oranges
1 kg/2¼ lb/5 cups granulated
  sugar
2 tsp white wine yeast

Makes about 6 x 75 cl bottles

Gather the dandelions on a sunny day, when you have time to use them right away. You will need a 4.5 litre/ 1 gallon/4½ quart demijohn, a siphoning tube and some wine yeast, available from home-brewing suppliers. Sterilize the brewing equipment with Campden tablets or Milton fluid.

1 Cut off any green parts of the flowers and place them in a large non-reactive bowl – if you don't want 'nicotine-stained' fingers, wear rubber gloves. Pour the boiling water over the flowers, cover with a clean cloth and leave to steep for 2 days.

2 Pare the zest off the oranges in wide strips, taking care to avoid the white pith, and add to the dandelion mixture. Pour it into a large saucepan, bring to the boil and simmer for 10 minutes.

3 Put the sugar into a large bowl, strain the dandelion mixture onto it and stir to dissolve the sugar. Leave to cool completely.

4 Squeeze the orange juice and add to the cooled mixture. Add the yeast, following the directions on the pack, and stir thoroughly. Pour into a 4.5 litre/1 gallon/4½ quart sterilized demijohn and if needed top up with cool boiled water, then seal with an airlock. Put the demijohn on a tray, in case the liquid bubbles over during the fermentation process. It will take a couple of months to ferment.

5 Once the fermentation has stopped, siphon the wine into a clean demijohn, seal with a cork and leave it in a cool cellar or garage for 6 months. Bottle and store for at least another 6 months before you drink it.

Dandelion Marmalade

This 'marmalade' contains shreds of dandelion petals and has an excellent, slightly bitter flavour, reminiscent of citrus marmalade. It gives a soft set, but if you want a firmer set, use jam sugar (with added pectin). You could also follow the recipe for Crab Apple Jelly (see page 133) and add the dandelion petals to the crab apples as you cook them.

1 kg/2¼ lb tart dessert apples,
   or a mix of dessert and baking
   apples, roughly chopped
85 g/3 oz dandelion petals
100 ml/3½ fl oz/6–7 tbsp freshly
   squeezed lemon juice
750 g/1 lb 10 oz/3¾ cups
   granulated sugar or jam sugar
   (with added pectin)

1 Put the apples in a pan with 600 ml/20 fl oz/2½ cups water and 55 g/2 oz of the dandelion petals and bring to just below boiling point. Remove from the heat, cover and leave to infuse overnight.

2 Strain the liquid to remove the apple pieces and petals, return it to the pan and add the lemon juice and sugar. Stir over a low heat until the sugar has dissolved, then add the remaining dandelion petals. Boil rapidly until setting point is reached (see page 10) – bear in mind that if you are not using jam sugar, the set will be soft.

3 Using a large spoon, remove any scum from the surface, then pour into warm, sterilized jars and seal immediately. If the petals are floating to the top, shake the jar once it is at room temperature to distribute the petals throughout the marmalade.

Wild Roses

Wild roses are common throughout the British Isles in hedgerows, scrub and municipal plantings. Dog roses are usually pink whereas field roses are always white. Both flower from early to mid summer, and the flowers are followed by the hips, which can be found until November. The Japanese rose is also common, especially near the coast. It has distinctive, dark pink, extremely fragrant flowers and huge hips, often on the bush at the same time as the flowers.

Rose petals are delightfully scented and make exotic jams and sweetmeats. Like other edible wild flowers, they can be crystallized to make a gorgeous and unusual decoration for cakes, trifles and jellies. To do this, coat each petal separately in lightly whipped egg white, dip in caster sugar and leave to set. The crystallized petals can be stored in an airtight container for up to 2 months.

The other real treasure is the hips. They can be harvested as soon as they have been softened by the first frost of autumn. Rose hips are rich in vitamin A and are said to contain more vitamin C than blackcurrant or orange juice. They are actually an extension of the stem and contain tiny fruits, which are covered in hairs. Mischievous children know these as itching powder, but don't worry, you will remove them by straining the hips after cooking.

Rose Petal Jam

Makes 3 large jars

1.5 litres/about 3 pints/6 cups wild rose petals (pressed down lightly in the measuring jug)
1 kg/2¼ lb/5 cups granulated sugar
3 lemons
Few drops of rosewater (optional)

The merest whiff of this delectable treat transports Ginny back to her childhood in Istanbul, where it is widely eaten on bread, stirred into yogurt or spooned over ice cream. We really enjoy it with croissants and other soft and slightly sweet breads for a weekend breakfast treat. The jam is a wonderful orangey-pink colour, even when made with pale pink dog roses, and has a lovely syrupy texture. Once you have made it we confidently predict you will become addicted to it as well.

1 Rinse and dry the rose petals. Put the rose petals in a bowl, sprinkle over the sugar and leave to macerate overnight. However, if you are short of time you can skip this stage and it will still be good.

2 Using a small sharp knife, cut the skin off the lemons, taking care to remove all the pith and holding them over a bowl to collect the juice.

3 Put the rose petals and sugar, lemon flesh and juice into a large saucepan or preserving pan together with 850 ml/1½ pints/3½ cups water and stir over a low heat until the sugar has dissolved completely. Then increase the heat and boil rapidly, without stirring. You will need to boil until the temperature is comfortably above normal jam setting point – closer to 110°C/230°F on a jam thermometer – and the colour will change slightly from pink to a more orangey hue. Test for set (see page 10), and as long as it is wrinkling a little it will be ready: this is a loose-set jam and it doesn't get very firm. Taste and if you prefer a stronger rose flavour than that provided by your petals alone, now is the moment to add a little rosewater. Once ready, leave to stand for 10 minutes, then pour into warm, sterilized jars and seal immediately.

Wild Rose Turkish Delight

Real Turkish delight is a wondrous treat with its flowery aroma, gorgeous colours and delicate flavour. If you can bear to part with any, it makes a fantastic gift and it is much easier to make than you might think, although you will need to allow 2 days for it to set fully. The pistachios are, whatever Ginny may say, optional. She is right, though, that they add delightful colour, flavour and texture.

Makes 64 pieces

Turkish Delight:
1.5 litres/about 3 pints/6 cups wild rose petals (pressed down lightly in the measuring jug)
700 g/1 lb 9 oz/3½ cups granulated sugar
Juice of 2 lemons
12 leaves of gelatine
140 g/5 oz/1 cup cornflour (cornstarch)
100 g/3½ oz/¾ cup shelled pistachios (optional)

To Dust:
40 g/1½ oz/5 tbsp icing (confectioners') sugar
40 g/1½ oz/5 tbsp cornflour (cornstarch)

1 Rinse the rose petals to remove any insects that may be hiding among the petals. Cut out a square of muslin (cheesecloth), pile the petals in the middle and tie up into a giant 'teabag' with some string, leaving a long end of string to hook the teabag out of the hot mixture later. Cut off any excess muslin, as it will just get in the way.

2 Put the granulated sugar, lemon juice and 300 ml/10 fl oz/1¼ cups water in a large saucepan or preserving pan and heat gently until the sugar has just dissolved, then remove from the heat and leave to cool for at least 5 minutes.

3 Soak the gelatine in cold water for about 5 minutes to soften. In a separate bowl, mix the cornflour with 100 ml/3½ fl oz/7 tablespoons water until smooth.

4 Squeeze out the excess water from the gelatine leaves one by one and whisk them into the lemon syrup, until completely dissolved. Then pour in the cornflour mixture and stir thoroughly. Put the pan over a medium heat and add the bag of rose petals. Don't worry that it seems huge: it will shrink dramatically as the petals get hot. Bring the mixture to the boil and simmer for 15 minutes, stirring frequently and squishing the bag from time to time to make sure you extract maximum flavour. As the cornflour cooks, the mixture will become a little less opaque. It will also become pretty thick and potentially explosive, so make sure you keep stirring.

5 Pull out the bag of rose petals and leave everything to cool for 10 minutes. Wearing rubber gloves, squeeze out as much of the rosy residue as possible from the muslin bag and add it back into the pan. Add the pistachio nuts, if using, and stir. Leave to cool slightly, until the pistachios remain in suspension, rather than rising to the top.

6 Line a 20 cm/8 inch square cake tin with baking parchment and pour in the Turkish delight. Leave to cool, uncovered. When cold, put in the fridge overnight.

7 The next day, cut the Turkish delight into squares and leave the individual squares to dry out on a wire rack for at least 12 hours. It is really important that the squares are utterly dry, otherwise they will partially absorb the dusting powder and become damp and sticky and most unattractive.

8 To dust, mix the cornflour and icing sugar together and toss the dry, rubbery squares in the mixture to coat evenly. Store in jars or gift boxes lined with baking parchment. It will keep for up to a month.

Rosehip Syrup

1 kg/2¼ lb rose hips
Juice of 2 lemons
400 g/14 oz/2 cups
   granulated sugar

Makes about
1½ litres/2¾ pints/
6½ cups

In Britain during the Second World War this was consumed in vast quantities to combat a diet lacking in vitamins from fresh fruit and vegetables. Possibly as a result, rosehip syrup has fallen out of favour since. This is a shame because it makes a fantastic sauce for ice cream and can be used in panna cotta and trifle as well being delicious to drink, diluted to taste. Adam Gildea, son of a good friend of ours and a committed forager, suggests diluting 50:50 with water and then freezing as lollipops. Utter bliss on a hot summer's day.

1 Wash the rose hips and roughly chop in a food processor. Put them into a large saucepan with 1.5 litres/2¾ pints/6¼ cups water and simmer gently until the hips are very soft. Remove from the heat and leave to stand for 15 minutes. Tip the mixture into a jelly bag or a sieve lined with muslin (cheesecloth) and leave it to drip into a large bowl for at least 1 hour.

2 Rinse out the pan and return the rosehip juice to the pan, add the lemon juice and sugar and stir over a low heat until the sugar has dissolved completely. Increase the heat and boil rapidly for a few minutes, then pour into warm, sterilized bottles and seal.

3 This syrup will keep for up to 4 months. If you would like to keep it for up to a year, follow the water bath sterilization method (see page 11).

Rosehip & Vanilla Jelly

Rosehip syrup and creamy vanilla are a combination made in heaven. And this pud makes a delightfully unusual contribution to a buffet table. It can be scaled up, depending on the size of your jelly mould, or it can be made as individual jellies. For this recipe you will need a jelly mould with a capacity of 600 ml/20 fl oz/2½ cups, and you will need to start the day before you want to eat it.

6 leaves of gelatine
225 ml/8 fl oz/scant 1 cup rosehip syrup (as left)
Touch of natural red food colouring (optional)
150 ml/5 fl oz/⅔ cup double (heavy) cream
150 ml/5 fl oz/⅔ cup semi-skimmed (lowfat) milk
30 g/1 oz/2 tbsp granulated sugar
Drop of vanilla extract

1 Start by soaking three of the gelatine leaves in cold water. Put the rosehip syrup and 75 ml/2½ fl oz/5 tbsp water in a saucepan and bring just to the boil. Remove the pan from the heat. Squeeze out the excess water from the gelatine leaves and drop them one at a time into the rosehip mixture, whisking briefly between each one, until completely dissolved. Assess whether you are happy with the colour of your jelly. We found that the gelatine took something away from the rosehip colour, which we wanted to put back – so we added a tiny amount (not even a drop) of natural red food colouring. Pour the mixture into your jelly mould. When it is cool enough, transfer it to the fridge. Leave for about 4 hours, or until it is very cold and firm.

2 Now it is time to make the vanilla jelly. Soak the remaining three gelatine leaves in cold water. In a small pan, mix together the cream, milk, sugar and vanilla and bring to the boil over a low heat, stirring from time to time, until the sugar has dissolved. As the mixture starts to boil, remove the pan from the heat and whisk in the squeezed-out gelatine leaves. Leave in the pan to cool until it is only just lukewarm. Then skim off any skin and pour the mixture gently on top of the rosehip jelly. Replace in the fridge and leave to set for 6 hours, or overnight.

3 To serve, dip the jelly mould in hot water for a few seconds and then invert it onto a pretty serving plate. It may need a bit of a shake to get it out. Then let it wobble with pride!

Leaves

There must be hundreds or even thousands of types of edible leaves growing wild around us, which we could eat if we had to – and doubtless our ancestors did. However, this is not a survival book, so we have restricted ourselves to a few kinds of greenery that are reasonably widespread, good to eat and easy to identify. We became very aware when writing this book how few British or Irish recipes exist for wild leaves and how very much appreciated they are in Italian, French and even Turkish cookery. Britain was the world's first industrial and urban nation; today we have the world's most concentrated supermarket sector – and for whatever reason, we have become less connected to the land, in a food sense, than our neighbours. However, we hope this collection of recipes encourages you to experiment.

The image shows a stinging nettle.

Wild Garlic or Ramsons

Wild garlic is common throughout Britain, growing in shady woodlands, often close to bluebells. The plants have beautiful white flowers that appear from April to June. They are slightly more delicate than a cultivated allium, but we cannot recommend them as cut flowers unless you have a very large and airy room, as their 'perfume' can be less than lovely! Anyhow, from a culinary perspective, it's primarily the leaves you want, ideally in March before the flowers appear, as they become tougher then. In fact, the flowers and the underground 'bulbs' are also edible, but it seems a shame to take the former (though they do make a good fritter, dipped whole in tempura batter – see page 21 – and deep-fried) and it's illegal to dig up wild roots unless you have the landowner's permission. Best to stick to the leaves, we say.

Positive identification is important, as ramson leaves can be confused with a number of seriously poisonous plants, such as lily of the valley, lords and ladies and autumn crocus. Happily there is an easy way to verify your find, as wild garlic smells powerfully garlicky, especially when crushed between your fingers. In fact, the smell is probably how you will find it in the first place.

Lately, wild garlic has become quite fashionable in smart restaurants. And no wonder, because it is a superb ingredient, with a flavour somewhere between spring onion and garlic. The leaves make a highly superior vegetable or can be used like a herb. Finely chop them and add to mayonnaise, to a salad, or to a tomato sauce instead of basil. In fact, once you have grown accustomed to using it, we're sure you will find any number of dishes that can be enhanced by this versatile leaf. When you find a wild garlic patch, we recommend greedily stuffing a supermarket bag with leaves. Don't worry, you will find uses for it, and anyway, once washed and stashed in the fridge, we've found the leaves will last for a month.

Wilted Ramsons

This is a really good vegetable to accompany roast lamb or chicken. It is savoury, slightly sweet and mildly oniony/garlicky.

250 g/9 oz wild garlic leaves
30 g/1 oz/2 tbsp butter
Salt and pepper

1 Wash the leaves and cut them into strips across the grain. Put the leaves, butter and 8 tbsp water in a pan and bring to the boil. Cook over a medium-high heat until the water has evaporated and the leaves are beautifully shiny. Season to taste and serve.

Wild Garlic Pesto

Wild garlic pesto is a wonderful thing. It is a fabulous standby, as it can be kept in the fridge and slung into soups and dressings to jazz them up. Obviously, it also makes a good sauce for gnocchi or pasta, and it is great with pinkly grilled spring lamb or pan-fried fillet of fish, although for fish you may want to omit the cheese.

70 g/2½ oz wild garlic leaves
50 g/1¾ oz pine nuts or walnuts
50 g/1¾ oz fresh Parmesan or other
  strong, hard cheese, finely grated
Juice of ½ lemon
About 100 ml/3½ fl oz/6–7 tbsp olive
  oil, plus 1 tbsp to cover
Salt and pepper

1 Heat the oven to 100°C/212°F/less than gas mark ¼ and put in your jar and lid to sterilize for 10 minutes. Remove from the oven and leave to cool slightly.

2 Put the wild garlic, nuts, cheese and lemon juice into a food processor and blitz for a few seconds. Then blitz again, adding the oil through the tube in a thin stream until the pesto reaches your desired consistency. Season to taste, then pour into the sterilized jar and cover with a little more olive oil, put the lid on and store in the fridge for up to 2 weeks.

Steak with Wild Garlic Butter

30 g/1 oz wild garlic leaves
140 g/5 oz/generous ½ cup butter,
  softened
Grated zest of 1 lemon
Salt and pepper

Enough for 4 people

We are going to assume here that you know what kind of steak you like and how you like it cooked. We are divided on this ourselves, so will not presume. Consequently, this recipe is just for the butter, which is also gorgeous used to dress spring vegetables or grilled fish, or spread generously under the skin of a chicken before roasting. The flavour is just lovely!

1 Wash and finely chop the garlic leaves, then use a fork to mash them into the butter with the lemon zest. Season with salt and pepper to taste. Roll the butter between two pieces of damp greaseproof (wax) paper to form a sausage shape and put it in the fridge for a couple of hours to firm up.

2 When your steak is cooked to perfection, take the garlic butter out of the fridge and place a generous slice on top, so that it can melt and combine with the steak juices as you eat.

3 The butter can be kept in the fridge for up to 3 weeks, or frozen.

Sweet Onion & Wild Garlic Tart

This is one of those recipes that came together one glorious lunchtime, whipped up by Caro out of the remnants in her fridge and a few wild garlic leaves picked on a walk. It was memorably good.

Pastry:
175 g/6 oz/1½ cups wholemeal plain (whole wheat all-purpose) flour
50 g/1¾ oz/4 tbsp cold butter, cubed
40 g/1½ oz/3 tbsp cold lard, cubed
Pinch of salt

Filling:
55 g/2 oz/4 tbsp butter
4 large white onions, finely sliced
Salt and pepper
About 40 wild garlic leaves, shredded
4 eggs
300 ml/10 fl oz/1¼ cups single (light) cream
Nutmeg, freshly grated
100 g/3½ oz soft goat's cheese (not too mild)

1 To make the pastry, put all the ingredients in a bowl and rub the fat into the flour (or blitz in a food processor) until the mixture resembles fine breadcrumbs. Gradually add 3 tablespoons cold water and stir with a knife until it starts to clump into large crumbs. Use your hands, or the food processor, to bring it together into a ball.

2 Roll out the pastry thinly on a floured surface. Line a tart tin about 24 cm/9½ inches in diameter, leaving some pastry overhanging. Prick the pastry all over with a fork and put it in the freezer for 20 minutes. (If you are using a ceramic dish, put it into the fridge for about 30 minutes.)

3 Preheat the oven to 200°C/400°F/gas mark 6. If the pastry is frozen or well chilled, you should not have to fiddle about with lining it. Bake the pastry for about 15 minutes or until lightly coloured.

4 Meanwhile, to make the filling, melt the butter in a large saucepan over a low-medium heat. Add the sliced onions and season quite generously with salt, to help draw out the moisture. Continue to cook, stirring occasionally, for about 30 minutes or until the onions have completely collapsed, are soft, golden and quite sweet. Test them before you stop cooking to check they have absolutely no 'bite' left in them. Add the shredded garlic leaves, stir briefly so that they wilt, then remove the pan from the heat.

5 Beat the eggs lightly in a bowl. Add the cream and season with salt, pepper and nutmeg to taste. Pour this over the onions and stir everything together. Tip the custard into the pastry shell and dot it with blobs of goat's cheese.

6 Bake the filled tart for 30–35 minutes, until the custard is risen round the edges but not in the centre of the tart – it should be almost set. Leave to cool for 15 minutes or so before serving with a crisp green salad.

Sorrel

A relative of rhubarb, common sorrel can be found in fields and hedgerows nearly everywhere in the British Isles for most of the year. It grows as a single-stemmed spike with reddish flowers and seeds at the top. The leaves are probably at their best in the spring: tender, young ones can be picked from February

However, unlike cultivated sorrel, which has a lovely, clean, lemony sourness, the common wild variety tends toward bitterness, which is good only in small quantities, and when teamed with other, more rounded, flavours. Our experience of wild sorrel has not made us into great fans. We therefore offer you just one recipe, and would recommend sticking to cultivated sorrel for delicate egg and fish dishes.

Sorrel's sour taste comes from oxalic acid, which in large quantities can be poisonous. In moderation and from time to time, it will do you no harm. However, do not cook sorrel in aluminium or cast-iron cookware, which can be damaged by its acidity.

Another word of warning: sorrel (of any kind) needs only the briefest amount of cooking. As soon as it comes into contact with serious heat, it exchanges its lovely bright green colour for a rather unflattering khaki. Are we selling this to you?!

Serves 6–8

Sorrel & Smoked Trout Tart with a Couscous Crust

This tart is unbelievably savoury and satisfying – and the virtuous couscous crust compensates for all the cheese and cream. (Bet you don't believe the crust holds together, do you? We couldn't believe it either to begin with, but honest, it does!)

Couscous Crust:
15 g/½ oz/1 tbsp butter, melted, for brushing
125 g/4½ oz/¾ cup couscous
Pinch of salt

Filling:
200 g/7 oz hot-smoked trout
30 g/1 oz/2 tbsp butter
100 g/3½ oz sorrel leaves, stalks and ribs removed
3 eggs
300 ml/10 fl oz/1¼ cups single (light) cream
100 g/3½ oz Parmesan or strong cheddar cheese, grated
Salt and pepper

1 Preheat the oven to 180°C/350°F/gas mark 4. Brush a 24 cm/9½ inch diameter tart tin with the melted butter.

2 Cook the couscous as directed on the pack. Add a pinch of salt. While it is still warm, put it into the tart tin and press it over the bottom and up the sides of the tin, using the back of a spoon. It doesn't matter if it is really thin on the bottom, but it should be thicker on the sides, so that the grains go all the way up. Put it in the fridge to firm up for 30 minutes if you have time.

3 To make the filling, flake the smoked trout over the bottom of the tart. Melt the butter in a saucepan, add the sorrel and cook until just wilted.

4 In a bowl, mix together the eggs, cream and cheese. Add the sorrel, taste and adjust the seasoning and pile everything into the tart on top of the trout. Bake for 30–40 minutes or until set and browned on top. Serve warm, with a tomato salad.

Nettles

AKA stinging nettles! But don't worry, you can pick them with rubber gloves on, using a pair of scissors, and once cooked they no longer bite. The important thing is to make sure you collect only the youngest, tenderest leaves from the top of the plant. Nettles can be gathered from March, but don't pick any more once you see flowers appearing. The leaves then become coarse and bitter, due to a chemical change, which is not good for you. Nettles are easy for most people to identify (see photograph page 34) and are likely to be confused only with dead-nettles (with flowers and no sting), which are also edible.

Nettles may be something of a wild superfood, as they are rich in vitamins A and C and contain lots of iron, potassium, calcium and even protein. In the past they have been used medicinally in many ways; today they are used to treat various urinary tract issues, hay fever and in creams for joint pain, strains and insect bites. Caro's grandmother, who lived hale and hearty to the age of 97, attributed her good health to a daily cup of nettle tea...though she did insist on a daily glass of stout, too!

Nettles must be our most ubiquitous wild herb, yet in the British Isles we rarely eat them nowadays, which is a shame. They taste a bit like spinach, though spinach is undoubtedly superior. But their chief culinary virtue is their vibrant, green colour, which does not fade on cooking.

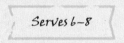

Serves 6–8

Nettle Soup

When we were at university, a hard-up friend thought she had found the ideal, frugal solution for dinner when it was her turn to feed her housemates. She had her eye on the luxuriant nettle patch that was their back garden, and spent a delightfully domestic afternoon converting it into a hearty, nutritious soup. Her friends – all men – tucked in on their return to the house, but were appalled when she revealed the contents of the soup. It turned out there was a very good reason for the nettles' luxuriant foliage: they had been regularly 'fertilized' by the boys on their return from the pub! Notwithstanding this story, soup is definitely one of the best things to make with nettles.

500 g/1 lb 2 oz nettle leaves
8 slices of streaky bacon
55 g/2 oz/4 tbsp butter
1 large onion, roughly chopped
1 leek, washed and sliced into rings
1 large potato, peeled and cut into dice
1 litre/1¾ pints/4 cups chicken or
    other light stock
Salt and pepper
2 tbsp crème fraîche or Greek yogurt

1 Wearing rubber gloves, wash the nettle leaves and remove any thick stalks. Drain.

2 Fry or grill the bacon until crisp and then chop into small pieces. Set aside.

3 Melt the butter in a saucepan, add the onion and leek and cook over a low heat until soft and sweet. Add the nettles, potato and stock and bring to the boil, then turn the heat down and simmer for about 15 minutes or until the potato is soft.

4 Whizz the soup in a blender or food processor until smooth and season with salt and pepper to taste. Serve with a swirl of crème fraîche or Greek yogurt and scatter the crisp bacon pieces over the top.

Nettle Beer

1 kg/2¼ lb nettle tops (one carrier
**   bag stuffed to bursting)**
Copper finings (optional)
450 g/1 lb/2¼ cups granulated sugar
1 sachet (1–2 tsp) of beer yeast
Juice of 2 lemons
55 g/2 oz cream of tartar

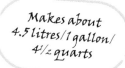

Makes about
4.5 litres/1 gallon/
4½ quarts

Beer has been made for centuries in Britain, using many different plants. This nettle beer is more like a light, easy-drinking sparkling wine than a beer and is ideal for serving chilled on a summer evening. It is quite alcoholic, but if you want to reduce its impact somewhat, add less sugar.

Many thanks to John Wright, author of *Hedgerow, River Cottage Handbook No. 7,* for this recipe. You will need a food-grade plastic bucket, a siphoning tube and some plastic or swing-top bottles, all of which should be sterilized with Campden tablets or Milton fluid. Any strange-sounding kit or ingredients are available from home-brewing suppliers. The finings are made from seaweed (though confusingly commonly sold as Irish moss!) and if you use them they should prevent the protein haze that may otherwise spoil the beer's appearance (though it must be said that, once opened, the fizz ensures this beer is less than crystal clear anyhow).

1 In a very large pan, boil the nettles in 5 litres/9 pints/5 quarts water with the finings, if using, for 15 minutes, stirring occasionally. Strain through a sieve into a sterilized plastic bucket. Stir in the sugar until dissolved, then leave to cool to room temperature (approximately 21°C/70°F).

2 Activate the yeast as directed on the pack. Add the yeast, lemon juice and cream of tartar to the bucket, stir, then cover with a clean cloth and leave to ferment for 4 days at room temperature.

3 Skim off any scum and siphon the beer into sterilized bottles, making sure not to disturb any sediment at the bottom of the bucket. As with Elderflower Champagne (see page 16) we recommend using heavy-duty plastic bottles with screw-top lids. The beer will continue to ferment and will be ready to drink in about a week, though it will improve if left for 2–3 weeks.

4 From time to time, say every 2 or 3 days, gently release the pressure that may have built up in the bottles by loosening the lids very gently and then tightening them again. If you forget to do this, beware of possible explosions!

5 When the sun is shining and you are ready to drink your beer, make sure you open the bottles over the sink. We have found this beverage has an alarming tendency to want to escape from the bottle when you open it! We think it is best served in a tall glass with a lump of sugar, a couple of ice cubes and a sprig of mint.

Casserole:
30 g/1 oz/2 tbsp butter
2 large onions, chopped
2 celery sticks, chopped
8 large rabbit pieces or 4 chicken
    legs, on the bone
2 tbsp plain (all-purpose) flour
1–2 tbsp vegetable oil
400 ml/14 fl oz/scant 1¾ cups
    dry or medium-dry cider
A generous sprig of thyme or
    some dried thyme
2 bay leaves
1 garlic clove, crushed
2 tbsp Dijon mustard
Salt and pepper
2 tbsp crème fraîche (optional)

Nettle Dumplings:
85 g/3 oz nettle tops, washed
115 g/4 oz self-raising flour
1 tsp baking powder
55 g/2 oz shredded suet
Salt and pepper

Serves 4

Rabbit Casserole with Nettle Dumplings

We really should eat more rabbits, since the countryside is practically overrun with them. Plus they are very low in fat and tasty, too. However, we know that not everyone can bear the thought of eating bunnies, and for others the bones are just too irritatingly fiddly. Never fear – this can be made with chicken legs if you prefer. Either way, we promise it is delicious.

Nettle pudding is supposedly Britain's oldest recipe, dating from about 6000 BC. We feel certain that those Ancient Britons would have teamed their pudding with a rabbit if one had been to hand, so these dumplings are dedicated to them, though we can't really vouch for their authenticity!

1 Preheat the oven to 160°C/325°F/gas mark 3.

2 Heat the butter in a frying pan (skillet) and cook the onions and celery over a medium heat until the onions are soft and translucent. Tip them out and set aside. Add the oil to the pan. Coat the rabbit or chicken pieces in flour and brown them all over in the hot oil. Remove and place in a casserole dish, together with the onions and celery. Deglaze the frying pan with a good splash of the cider, then pour into the casserole dish and add the thyme, bay leaves, garlic, mustard, salt and pepper. Cover with a lid and cook in the oven for about 1¼ hours, until the rabbit is tender.

3 Remove the casserole from the oven and fish out the bay leaves and thyme branch, which will have lost most of its leaves. If there seems to be too much sauce, remove some and reduce it in a pan over medium-high heat. Return it to the casserole and add the crème fraîche, if using.

4 While the rabbit is cooking, prepare the nettles and make the dumplings. Throw the nettles into a hot pan with a little boiling water and blanch them for about 1–2 minutes. Drain the nettles and plunge them into a bowl of cold water to help retain their beautiful colour. Drain well, then roll them up in a clean tea towel and wring out the moisture by turning each end in opposite directions. Chop the nettles roughly into small pieces, but not into a purée.

5 In a mixing bowl, mix the flour, baking powder, suet, salt and pepper to taste and chopped nettles. Add just enough cold water to allow you to form the mixture into 8–12 balls – keep the mixture as dry as you can, because more moisture will come out of the nettles as they cook.

6 Place the dumplings in a circle on top of the rabbitty mixture. Replace the lid and put the casserole dish back in the oven for 20–30 minutes, until the dumplings are light and puffy. Serve at once.

Turkish Nettle & Feta Filo Pastries (Börek)

When Ginny was young, she lived in Istanbul and attended the 'English High School for Girls', a terrible misnomer, since she and her sister were practically the only English children there and most of the pupils were boys! The food served at lunchtime was very Turkish and has left both sisters with an abiding passion for 'börek', which are luckily very easy to make (though even easier to eat). Serve as part of a mezze, or 2–3 each as a starter, 4–5 as a main course. You can replace some or all of the nettles with spinach if you prefer.

Makes about 25 börek

125 g/4½ oz nettle leaves, washed
200 g/7 oz feta cheese, crumbled
2 eggs, beaten
2 generous tbsp plain yogurt
Handful of fresh mint leaves, shredded
½ tsp salt
Freshly ground black pepper
100 g/3½ oz/7 tbsp butter
5–6 sheets of ready-made filo pastry

1 Blanch the nettles in boiling water for 1–2 minutes. Drain thoroughly and chop roughly.

2 Put the crumbled feta cheese, eggs, yogurt, mint and chopped nettles into a bowl. Season with salt and pepper to taste and mix everything together thoroughly.

3 Preheat the oven to 180°C/350°F/gas mark 4. Butter two baking sheets, or line them with baking parchment.

4 Melt the butter in a small pan. Unroll a sheet of filo pastry and cover the rest with clingfilm (plastic wrap), to prevent it from drying out. Turn the filo sheet so that the longest edges are at top and bottom and brush it sparingly with butter. Then, depending on the width of your filo, cut it vertically into 5 or 6 strips, each about 7–8 cm/3 inches wide.

5 Take one strip of filo and put a teaspoon of the nettle and feta mixture 2–3 cm/1 inch from the top. Working quickly, flip the filo over in triangles, to fully encase the mixture. When you get to the end of each strip, put the triangular börek onto one of the baking sheets. Brush with butter to stop the pastry drying out. Continue until you have used up all the mixture. We think you will be surprised by how speedy this becomes once you have practised on one or two.

6 At this stage, you can freeze some or all of the börek if you wish. They cook well from frozen and make a useful impromptu lunch item. However, assuming you want to eat at least some now, bake in the oven for 15 minutes or until golden and crisp. Serve while still warm with good bread and a peasant salad (*çoban salatasi*) of chopped ripe tomatoes, peeled cucumber, green peppers, red onions and lots of chopped flat-leaf parsley, simply dressed with a little wine vinegar, olive oil, salt and pepper. Mmmmmm!

Amazingly Green Pasta Ribbons (Strettine)

115 g/4 oz nettle tops
2 eggs
280 g/10 oz/2¼ cups Italian
 '00' pasta flour

Serves 4 as a
main course

The chief virtue of using nettles over spinach in pasta is the fabulous bright green colour. The flavour contribution of the nettles is negligible, much to the relief of our fussy teenagers, who found this 'all right, actually' (high praise!). This is an Italian springtime favourite, which can be dressed up or down. It's great with a mushroomy, gamy ragù, with your favourite tomato sauce or simply tossed in foaming butter and scattered with fresh Parmesan. It can also be turned into ravioli if you can be bothered. Our opinion regarding pasta-making is that unless you have a pasta machine, don't. It's way too hard to get it right!

1 Blanch the nettles in a pan of boiling, salted water for 1–2 minutes. Drain the nettles and plunge them into a bowl of cold water to help retain their beautiful colour. Drain in a colander, then roll them up in a clean tea towel and wring out the moisture by turning each end in opposite directions. Squeeze out as much water as possible.

2 Put the nettles in a food processor and pulse until they are puréed. Add the eggs and blend again. Finally add the flour and pulse until it forms a ball. If it seems a little dry and crumbly, add a tiny bit of lukewarm water and pulse again. If it is too wet, add some more flour. Tip it all out of the food processor and knead for a couple of minutes or so until smooth. Shape it into a ball and wrap in clingfilm (plastic wrap). Leave it to rest for an hour.

3 Cut off a third of the dough, dust it with flour and put it through your pasta machine on progressively thinner settings, until it is the thickness you like. Then you can either cut the sheet of pasta into ribbons using the pasta machine's attachment or you can cut it by hand. If doing it by hand, you will need to dust the sheet of pasta with more flour and loosely roll it up. Using a sharp knife, slice the pasta at intervals of about 5 mm/¼ inch. Lay the noodles on a floured board and throw some more flour over them. Repeat with the rest of the dough.

4 The strettine will keep for a day or so, twisted up into loose nests and left to dry. However, they are best cooked on the day of making. Add to lots of boiling, salted water until they float. Cook for another minute or so, then drain and serve.

Marsh Samphire
or Glasswort

The name samphire is a corruption of 'Saint Pierre', the patron saint of fishermen, but this is a true seashore vegetable – *not* a seaweed. Marsh samphire is an annual that grows around the British coast, on open, sandy mud and on salt marshes, often in profusion in great meadows. It is rich in soda, hence its other name of 'glasswort', as it was commonly used in the making of glass and indeed soap.

There is a second, unrelated form of samphire, called rock samphire. It tastes different and grows in completely different environments to glasswort, ie cliffs and rocks. Since it is much rarer, we have chosen to focus on its marshy cousin.

Samphire can be gathered using a pair of scissors to snip the stems from the roots, so long as you are brave enough to don a pair of wellies and face the mud. Traditionally, it can be picked from Midsummer Day until August and the best plants are those that are washed daily by the sea, so you will need to go picking at low tide. And it is well worth your while! Not only do those crisp little stems have a deliciously complex, salty-savoury flavour, but as more and more people come to appreciate its culinary value, samphire has become ruinously expensive – if you can find it at all – in the fishmonger's.

Once home, samphire should be very thoroughly washed as soon as possible. It is best eaten the same day, but it will keep, wrapped in newspaper and kept in the fridge, for 4–5 days. Young plants can be eaten raw in salads or sandwiches. Samphire is famously known as 'sea asparagus' and it can be treated in much the same way: young samphire stems should be boiled in unsalted water for about a minute, before being drained and served with melted butter and lemon or hollandaise sauce. This is stunningly good with pan-fried fish.

Samphire Salads

Samphire makes a beautiful summer salad. Probably our favourite way of eating it is simply boiled and teamed with fresh crab, a big wedge of lemon, a dollop of good mayonnaise and lots of freshly ground black pepper. The salt and soda in the samphire contrast perfectly with the sweetness of the crab meat.

Alternatively, it makes a great salad in its own right. This is a Turkish recipe (*deniz borulcesi salatasi*) for garlicky, olive-oily samphire, which is good with some thick Greek yogurt, either as part of a salad selection or as a side dish with grilled fish or lamb.

500 g/1 lb 2 oz marsh samphire, cleaned
  and trimmed of any woody bits
2 tbsp freshly squeezed lemon juice
1–2 garlic cloves, sliced thinly
3 tbsp extra virgin olive oil

1 If the samphire is excessively salty, soak it in fresh cold water for 24–48 hours, changing the water at least once.

2 Bring a large pan of water to the boil. Do not add salt! Once it is boiling, add the samphire and bring back to the boil for about 1 minute, so that it is just cooked. Drain and briefly plunge it in cold water, to preserve its colour. Lift it out before it is completely cold. Whisk together the lemon juice, garlic and olive oil and dress the samphire while it is still slightly warm. Serve with crusty bread.

Pickled Samphire

300 g/about 10 oz marsh
  samphire, cleaned and trimmed
  of any woody bits
400 ml/14 fl oz/1¾ cups cider
  vinegar
5 black peppercorns
1 tsp mustard seeds
½ tsp fennel seeds
55 g/2 oz/¼ cup granulated sugar

Makes 2 large jam jars

We first came across pickled samphire in seaside shops in Brittany, where very scary-looking jars of dark khaki fronds were proudly displayed alongside even scarier jars of murky-looking fish soup. Now we are older and wiser and know to our cost that appearances can be deceptive, we understand that the shopkeepers were absolutely right to be proud of their wares. It is true that pickled samphire is not a beautiful colour – but it certainly is beautiful on the inside. And in spite of indications to the contrary, it does not taste of seaweed; it has a lovely crunch and a salt/sharp/sweet flavour all of its own.

Since the samphire season is relatively short, it is great to have a way of preserving some for use in the winter. In addition, we have found that once you find yourself on a samphire meadow, it is quite hard to stop picking when you have the right amount for tea – and it's such a shame to waste something so good.

1 If the samphire is particularly salty, soak it in fresh cold water for 24–48 hours, changing the water at least once. Young plants should not require this desalinating stage.

2 Meanwhile, make the pickling vinegar by putting all the other ingredients into a pan. Bring to the boil and then simmer for 5–10 minutes. Strain out all the spices and leave it to cool completely.

3 The next day, heat the oven to 100°C/212°F/less than gas mark ¼ and sterilize your jars and lids for 10 minutes. Remove from the oven and leave to cool slightly.

4 Bring a pan of water to the boil. When it is boiling vigorously, add the samphire and bring back to the boil for 60 seconds only. Drain immediately and plunge the samphire into a bowl of very cold water. This should maintain its lovely crunch. Once it is cold, drain and lay it out to dry on a clean tea towel for 30 minutes.

5 Pack the samphire into the sterilized jars, pour in the spiced vinegar and seal tightly. Sadly, after a few hours, the samphire will turn from a fabulously vibrant green to scary khaki. We think of it as the small price you have to pay in order to be able to eat samphire in the winter.

6 Keep for at least 3 weeks before opening. Use it as you might use cornichons, with pâté and cold meats or fish, for a little blast of salty, vinegary savouriness.

Rack of Salt-Marsh Lamb with Piquant Samphire

Since salt-marsh lamb and samphire come from the same places, this is surely a match made in heaven, the piquant samphire being a more appropriate accompaniment than mint sauce or jelly. However, if you do not have a ready supply of salt-marsh lamb, we can confirm that the samphire is also very good with grass-fed lamb!

Lamb:
2 tbsp vegetable oil
2 racks of lamb, weighing about 500 g/1 lb each (ask your butcher to French trim them and cut them in half – there should be 3 or 4 cutlets on each piece)
Salt and pepper

Piquant Samphire:
500 g/1 lb 2 oz marsh samphire, cleaned and trimmed (we know this looks a lot, but it really does shrink!)
2 tbsp cider vinegar
1 tbsp sugar
20 g/¾ oz/1½ tbsp butter

1 If the samphire is very salty, soak it in fresh cold water for 24–48 hours, changing the water at least once.

2 Preheat the oven to 200°C/400°F/gas mark 6.

3 Heat the oil in a frying pan (skillet). Season the lamb and cook over a high heat, turning to brown it all over (about 5 minutes in total). Transfer to a roasting pan and cook in the oven for 15 minutes, depending on the size of the racks and how you want them cooked. Remove from the oven and let them rest for 5 minutes.

4 Meanwhile, cook the samphire in a pan over a medium-high heat, just with the water that clings to it after washing/soaking. After a couple of minutes, add the vinegar, sugar and butter. Cook over a high heat until the juices start to smell slightly caramelized. Serve immediately, with the lamb and some new potatoes.

Dandelion Leaves

We have discussed dandelion flowers earlier in this book (see page 24), but the leaves of this incredibly common wild plant are also worth considering as food – although once the plant has started flowering the leaves are really too bitter to be used. In France they are often eaten young as a salad. Pick dandelion leaves from the centre of the plant and combine them with milder salad leaves. Add a warm poached egg and crispy bacon for a substantial dish, or dress lightly with cobnut or hazelnut oil, salt and pepper.

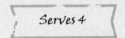
Serves 4

Dandelions with Veal

We would like to thank a good friend, Mary Birnie, for this recipe. Mary's grandmother, an Irish-American lady, married into an Italian-American clan, who were not at all keen on Irish food! So she set about collecting their favourite Italian recipes and this is tasty dish is one of them. In her journal, she describes how gathering the dandelions for this dish became a spring ritual, enjoyed by the whole family.

The chicory-style bitter note in the dandelions offsets the sweetness of the tomatoes and veal and lightens the dish. It makes a great lunch or supper and with pink (rose) veal so good and so underused, we thought you might like to try it. If you haven't time to collect your own dandelion leaves, you can use chicory (Belgian endive) or chard, instead.

2–3 tbsp olive oil
500 g/1 lb 2 oz stewing veal, cut into small pieces
1 large onion, chopped
400 g/14 oz can chopped tomatoes
1 green pepper, deseeded and diced
2 tsp sugar
½ tsp dried oregano
½ tsp dried basil
½ tsp fennel seeds, crushed
250 g/9 oz dandelion leaves, washed
Salt and pepper
4 eggs, beaten
55 g/2 oz pecorino (or Parmesan) cheese, grated

1 Preheat the oven to 180°C/350°F/gas mark 4. You will need a 2.5 litre/4½ pint/2½ quart casserole or lasagne dish: we used a lasagne dish measuring 20 x 24 cm/8 x 9½ inches.

2 Heat a little of the oil in a frying pan (skillet) and brown the veal. Remove it from the pan using a slotted spoon and place in the dish. Add a little more oil to the pan and cook the onion over a medium heat until softened and sweet, but not browned. Add to the veal.

3 Put the tomatoes, pepper, sugar, oregano, basil and fennel seeds into the dish, cover with a lid or foil and cook in the oven for 1–1½ hours, or until the veal is meltingly tender. Meanwhile, blanch the dandelion leaves in boiling water for 1–2 minutes, drain and set aside.

4 Taste the casserole and adjust the seasoning, then add the dandelions. Put the dish back into the oven for 5–10 minutes to heat through.

5 Remove from the oven and stir in the beaten eggs and most of the grated cheese. Sprinkle the remaining cheese on top and return the dish to the oven, uncovered, for a final 10–15 minutes, until the egg is a little puffy and the cheese is browned and crunchy.

6 Serve accompanied by a green salad and some crusty bread. We have been told this improves if you eat it the next day, but I'm afraid we never have any left, so can't vouch for that!

Berries

Berries are the most accessible of all wild foods. They are easy to identify and delicious to eat, either straight off the bush (as can be verified by countless parents of happy, pink-stained children) or in sophisticated, jewel-studded confections. Furthermore, most are rarely seen in shops and yet they appear in such glorious abundance in late summer that it's hard for many of us to resist the temptation to 'do something with them'. Transformed into jam, jelly or chutney, they will bring sunshine to your table in the depths of winter. So why resist?

The image shows wild blackberries.

Wild Strawberries

Common and native throughout the British Isles, except in the very north of Scotland, wild strawberries tend to grow in dry, grassy places and particularly on chalky soils. When fully ripe and rounded, they have a fragrance and flavour that is more delicate and intensely sweet than cultivated strawberries. However, we have a lot of competition from birds for these treasures and so most of the ones we pick tend to be half ripe.

Nothing transports us back to childhood like the sight of their tiny ruby berries – doll's house versions of the Brobdingnagian ones in the supermarket. Ginny's mother used to captivate us with wonderful stories of how her mother made little pots of wild strawberry jam during the Second World War, with sugar she had secretly saved from their ration. We made some recently, to try and recapture the experience, but it was very disappointing. The berries took hours to pick and the jam was impossibly pippy. We can imagine it was good in wartime, but the moment has probably passed.

If you manage to bring any home at all, we think it's best to showcase them in a decorative way, keeping them fresh and visible so people can enjoy their special flavour properly. They are pretty on top of a trifle or in a glass of sparkling wine, and this Pimm's jelly makes a real feature of them.

Pimm's Jelly

We are indebted to chef and food writer Mark Hix for this piece of inspiration, which looks and tastes like the distillation of a great British summer. It is best made in individual glasses and it is fabulous on a sunny day or after a barbecue, but don't make the mistake of giving any to your children!

1 large lemon
125 g/4½ oz/generous ½ cup caster (superfine) sugar
A few sprigs of mint, plus extra to decorate
Peel from ⅓ cucumber
Grated zest of ½ orange
4 leaves of gelatine
200 ml/7 fl oz/scant 1 cup Pimm's No. 1
150 g/5½ oz wild strawberries
A few borage flowers, if possible

1 Pare off the lemon zest in thin strips, avoiding the white pith. Squeeze the juice. Put 400 ml/14 fl oz/1¾ cups water in a saucepan and add the sugar, mint, cucumber peel, lemon zest and juice and orange zest. Bring to the boil and simmer gently for 2 minutes. Remove from the heat and leave to infuse for 1 hour. Strain though a fine sieve.

2 Soak the gelatine in cold water for 5 minutes to soften, then squeeze out the excess water. Bring about 100 ml/3½ fl oz/6–7 tbsp of the strained liquid back to the boil, add the gelatine leaves one at a time and stir until dissolved. Stir into the rest of the strained liquid, together with the Pimm's.

3 Pour the liquid into four glasses and add the strawberries and the borage flowers, if using. Place the glasses in the fridge to set for 5 hours or ideally overnight.

4 To serve, decorate with a sprig of fresh mint. It's really good with ice cream or whipped cream.

Blackberries or Brambles

Blackberries are the essence of late summer in Britain. They are the most plentiful of our wild fruit, found everywhere except the north of Scotland. (And we can't be sorry for the people there, as they have wild raspberries instead.) Even in our cities, bramble bushes thrive and tempt us with their shiny black fruits, bursting with sweet and sour juices. Surely everyone must have gone 'blackberrying' as a child, returning home sunkissed and scratched in equal measure, carrying a precious haul of perfumed fruit in an old plastic ice-cream tub. Today we always wear wellies, thick jeans and a long-sleeved shirt on these missions. We marvel at Ginny's dog, a Labrador with a passion for all things containing the merest hint of a calorie, who accompanies us and hoovers the berries off the barbed-wire bushes using only her soft mouth. Clever dog.

Blackberrying has remained a popular pastime, while foraging for many other wild foods is nowadays regarded as difficult or even dangerous. This is partly because of their profusion, and partly because it is almost impossible to mistake a blackberry for anything else; the only possible confusion is with the dewberry, which is very similar except it has fewer drupelets, is more blue-grey than black and has a more delicate flavour. Reassuringly, it is just as edible.

Blackberries come in a wide spectrum of flavours, ranging from lemony and mouth-puckeringly sour to subtly, fragrantly sweet. Apparently, this is because there are so many micro-species: over 400 in Britain alone. In addition, flavour can vary depending on whether you're picking the 'prime' berries from the end of each branch, which ripen first and which are the best ones to eat fresh, or the 'secondary' berries from the rest of the bush, which are supposedly best used for culinary purposes. As befits a food we have been eating for millennia, folklore also has something to say on the matter. You should not pick brambles after Michaelmas (either 29 September or 10 October, depending on which calendar you're following) because the devil will have spat on them, stamped on them – or worse! However, if we can find a good patch of fruit after this date, we count ourselves as lucky.

Happily – since they are so abundant that our families find it hard to stop picking them once we've started – there are many delicious foods to make from blackberries. We often return home with kilos of glittering black treasure, knowing full well they will not last, as mould spores invisibly cover their surfaces. However, brambles freeze well, for later use in pies, crumbles and smoothies. We also purée some and sieve out the pips, before freezing them in small tubs. This purée is great as an instant sauce or to use in ice creams and fools. But for us, the greatest pleasure of all is to make bramble jam or jelly with those mountains of heavenly fruit. Since starting Wild at Heart, we have found that it is almost impossible to buy British blackberries at a price that allows you to make a proper, fruity bramble jelly for anything approaching a commercial selling price. This rather tickles us, as it means the <u>only</u> way to have it on your breakfast toast is to make it yourself.

And one last reason, come August/September, to switch off the playstation and detach your kids from the TV: blackberries are <u>really</u> good for you. They are high in fibre, vitamin C, folic acid and antioxidants. Roll over, blueberry!

Bramble Jelly & Blackberry Seedless Jam

Makes 8–10 large jars of seedless jam, or about half as many of jelly

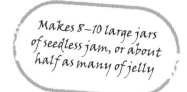

2 kg/4½ lb blackberries, washed
Juice of 2 large lemons
Approximately 2 kg/4½ lb/10 cups
   white granulated sugar

When is a blackberry a bramble? The books tell us that northerners call blackberries 'brambles'. However, Ginny grew up in West Sussex and as far as she's concerned, 'brambles' is what they are. Maybe having a Scottish mother has something to do with it. Anyhow, we think it's up to you.

You can make blackberry jam if you want to, but frankly, we don't think it justifies all those stings and scratches you've inevitably collected. The pips get in the way of pleasure. Jelly and seedless jam (or 'cheese') on the other hand are a real delight and only a little bit more work. Spread on toast or a warm scone, either will transport you back to harvest time. Caro's children love to mix bramble jelly into their porridge, turning it bright purple. Ginny's lot adore it with game: rabbit, venison, duck – anything, really!

Blackberries are low in pectin, which means it can be difficult to get the jelly to set, though we find the addition of lemon juice completely resolves the problem. Jane Grigson suggests that if you know you are going to use blackberries to make jelly, you should purposely pick a few red (unripe) ones to help with flavour and set. Maybe if your berries are from very late in the season, you might consider adding another lemon or two.

1 Put the berries in a large pan with the lemon juice and 500 ml/ 18 fl oz/2 cups water and simmer until the berries are soft and have given up their juice.

2 To make jelly, tip the mixture into a jelly bag or a sieve lined with muslin (cheesecloth) over a large bowl. Leave to drip overnight, or for 6 hours.

3 If you are less patient, or wish to extract the maximum amount of blackberry goodness from your haul, make seedless jam instead. Push the cooked blackberries and juice through a sieve, which will remove most of the seeds and leave you with a purée. Alternatively, use a food mill on the fine setting – the job will be infinitely easier.

4 Measure the juice or purée and return it to the cleaned pan. For every 500 ml/18 fl oz/2 cups of juice or purée, add 400 g/14 oz/ 2 cups sugar. Cook over a medium heat, stirring until all the sugar has dissolved. Increase the heat and boil rapidly, without stirring, testing for set every 5 minutes (see page 10) until setting point is reached. Once you are satisfied the jelly/jam will set, remove from the heat and skim off any scum. Ladle it into warm, sterilized jars and seal immediately.

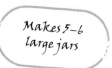

Makes 5–6 large jars

Bramble & Apple Jam with Cinnamon

This is for those of you who must have jam with proper pieces of fruit in it, rather than jelly, and it's practically foolproof – a good introduction to jam-making. The apple reduces the proportion of bramble seeds and adds a lovely texture, while the spices make it really special, though you can omit them if you wish. The jam is good as a filling for a Victoria sponge, along with a generous quantity of whipped cream. It adds a fabulous purple gash to the middle of the cake – not to mention a delicious flavour!

1 kg/2¼ lb mix of dessert and baking apples, peeled, cored and chopped into dice
1 kg/2¼ lb blackberries, washed
1.5 kg/3 lb 5 oz/7½ cups white granulated sugar
1–2 cinnamon sticks, depending on size
1 tsp grated nutmeg

1 Put all the ingredients into a heavy-bottomed pan. Cook gently and stir until all the sugar has dissolved and the mixture has become juicy. (Add a few drops of water if you're worried it's going to catch). Increase the heat and boil rapidly, stirring to ensure it is not sticking, until setting point is reached (see page 10). Spoon into warm, sterilized jars and seal.

500 g/1 lb 2 oz blackberries, washed
300 g/10½ oz cooking apples or windfalls, cored and diced (not peeled)
200 g/7 oz red onions, chopped
200 g/7 oz/1 cup white granulated sugar
70 g/2½ oz fresh root ginger, peeled and finely grated
2 tbsp Dijon mustard
½ tbsp black onion seeds
200 ml/7 fl oz/generous ¾ cup cider vinegar

Makes 2–3 large jars

Gorgeous Bramble Chutney

Quick, easy to make, inexpensive, a beautiful pinky-purple colour, fresh, fruity and absolutely delicious, this chutney is delightful with cheese, and is ready to eat as soon as it's cool. It has a mild heat from the ginger and mustard, which we think is perfect, but it can be enhanced by increasing the mustard and ginger by 50 per cent.

1 Combine all the ingredients in a large saucepan. Using a wooden spoon, stir over a medium heat until the sugar has dissolved. Turn up the heat and bubble, uncovered, for about 30 minutes.

2 To test if it is ready, draw your wooden spoon quickly across the bottom of the pan. If you can briefly glimpse the bottom, it is done. Ladle into warm, sterilized jars and seal. Serve with mature cheddar cheese or cold ham.

Bramble Sorbet & Ice Cream

These are two of the most delicious ways to eat blackberries we know. Try serving with a buttery apple tart, still warm from the oven, or team them with something darkly chocolatey. We promise, you won't be disappointed. Homemade sorbets and ice creams are incredibly easy once you have an ice-cream making machine: we strongly recommend putting one on your Christmas list.

Sorbet:
700 g/1 lb 9 oz blackberries
300 g/10½ oz/1½ cups granulated sugar
Juice of 2–4 lemons

Makes about 1 litre/1¾ pints/4 cups

1 Put the blackberries in a pan with 150 ml/5 fl oz/⅔ cup water and bring to the boil. Simmer for about 5 minutes, or until the berries are fully cooked. Briefly whizz the mixture with a handheld blender and then push it through a fine sieve, to remove those pesky seeds.

2 Add the sugar and the juice of 2 lemons to the purée, then taste it. Blackberries vary widely in acidity and flavour, so if you think the mixture lacks punch, you may want to add more lemon juice. Leave to cool and, if you have the time, chill in the fridge.

3 Pour into an ice-cream maker and churn according to the manufacturer's instructions. Alternatively, to freeze without an ice-cream maker, pour the mixture into a container and freeze, stirring briefly with a fork every 30 minutes to break up the ice crystals, until nearly firm. Charmingly, the sorbet turns from black to deep pink as it churns and air is incorporated into it. Scoop it into a 1 litre/1¾ pint/4 cup capacity container, cover and store in the freezer for up to 2 months. You may want to give it 15–20 minutes at room temperature before you serve it.

Makes about 1.2 litres/ 2 pints/5 cups

Ice Cream:
600 ml/20 fl oz/2½ cups single (light) cream
6 egg yolks
200 g/7 oz/1 cup caster (superfine) sugar
500 g/1 lb 2 oz blackberries

1 In a saucepan, gently heat the cream to simmering point. Meanwhile, in a food mixer, beat the egg yolks and sugar together until creamy and thick. Pour the hot cream over the yolk mixture in a thin stream, beating all the time to prevent the eggs from curdling. Return the mixture to the pan and heat until it starts to thicken, stirring continuously. Remove from the heat, cover with clingfilm (plastic wrap) to prevent a skin from forming and leave the custard somewhere it will become cold as quickly as possible.

2 Blitz the blackberries in a food processor, then push through a sieve to remove the seeds. Combine the purée with the custard. Churn in ice-cream maker or freeze, as for the sorbet recipe above.

Blackberry & Apple Crumble Cake

This cake manages to combine all our favourite autumn flavours in one, greedy bite: juicy, tart blackberries, sweet apples, crunchy hazelnuts and just a hint of cinnamon. It is great at teatime and also makes a good pudding.

Crumble Topping:
115 g/4 oz/½ cup butter
115 g/4 oz/scant 1 cup plain (all-purpose) flour
85 g/3 oz/⅔ cup hazelnuts, toasted, skinned and roughly chopped
115 g/4 oz/generous ½ cup soft brown sugar
½ tsp ground cinnamon

Cake:
150 g/5½ oz/generous ½ cup butter, softened
150 g/5½ oz/¾ cup caster (superfine) sugar
3 large eggs
85 g/3 oz/scant ¾ cup plain (all-purpose) flour
1½ tsp baking powder
115 g/4 oz/generous 1 cup ground almonds
1½ large dessert apples
200 g/7 oz blackberries

1 Preheat the oven to 180°C/350°F/gas mark 4. Line a 20 cm/ 8 inch diameter loose-bottomed or springform cake tin with baking parchment.

2 To make the crumble topping, melt the butter in a small saucepan, remove from the heat and mix in all the other ingredients. Set aside to cool.

3 To make the cake, cream the butter and sugar together in a food mixer until light and fluffy. Break the eggs, one at a time, into the bowl and beat well after each egg. If the mixture starts to curdle, add a spoonful of the flour to stabilize it. In a separate bowl, stir together the flour, baking powder and ground almonds. Carefully fold the flour mixture into the batter. Spoon into the cake tin, mounding it up slightly in the centre, as this cake has a bit of a tendency to sink in the middle.

4 Peel, core and quarter the apples. Chop each quarter into 6– 8 chunky pieces. Push the pieces gently into the top of the cake. Tumble the blackberries over the top and then tip the crumble onto the blackberries, aiming for a reasonably even distribution.

5 Bake for about 1 hour. It's ready when a skewer comes cleanly out of the cake's centre. Leave it in the tin for 10 minutes or so and then turn it out onto a wire rack to cool – or almost cool – before slicing and serving.

Bramble Fool

400 g/14 oz blackberries
125 g/4½ oz/½ cups granulated
    sugar
Juice of ½ lemon
300 ml/10 fl oz/1¼ cups double
    (heavy) cream
few drops of vanilla extract
250 g/9 oz/1 cup Greek yogurt –
    0% fat is fine

Serves 4

A very pretty pud for when the sun's shining. You can make the bramble purée when the blackberries are plentiful (to the end of stage 1) and stick it in the freezer. Then it is the work of moments to turn the purée into a beautiful pudding at any time of the year.

1 Pick out 12 pretty blackberries and set aside. Put the remaining blackberries in a saucepan with the sugar and 1 tablespoon water. Slowly bring to the boil over a low heat, until they are juicy. Push the mixture through a fine sieve or a food mill to remove the seeds. Add the lemon juice and leave to cool completely.

2 Whip the cream with the vanilla extract until soft peaks form. Fold in the yogurt and two-thirds of the purée, until just combined. Spoon the mixture into glasses and drizzle over the remaining blackberry purée. Decorate with the reserved berries and serve straightaway.

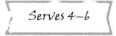
Old Fashioned Bramble Pudding

This is a great Sunday lunch crowd-pleaser. It's simple to make, so long as you remember to put it on to steam early enough – and it's surprisingly light. You can make it with 100 per cent blackberries, as here, or you can include pretty much whatever you come across in your morning walk. It's good with bilberries, elderberries, raspberries or even with damsons thrown in.

125 g/4½ oz/generous ½ cup butter, softened, plus extra for greasing
125 g/4½ oz/½ cup caster (superfine) sugar
2 eggs
125 g/4½ oz/1 cup self-raising flour
75 ml/2½ fl oz/5 tbsp milk
300 g/10½ oz blackberries
85 g/3 oz/scant ½ cup granulated sugar
150 ml/5 fl oz/⅔ cup red wine

1 Butter a 1.2 litre/2 pint/5 cup ovenproof pudding bowl or soufflé dish and line the bottom with a small disc of baking parchment. You will need a saucepan large enough to contain the bowl or dish and cover it with a lid. Pour 2–3 cm/about 1 inch of water into the pan.

2 Beat the butter and caster sugar together in a food mixer until light and fluffy. Beat in the eggs, one at a time, and then fold in the flour with the milk, until smooth.

3 Put about a third of the blackberries into the buttered bowl. Spoon the pudding mixture over the berries; it should come no higher than three-quarters of the way up the bowl. Cover the bowl with a piece of foil, pleated in the middle to allow room for expansion, and crunch the foil around the edge of the bowl to seal.

4 Bring the water in the saucepan to the boil, lower the pudding bowl into it and put the lid on. Reduce the heat so the water is just simmering. Steam for 1½–2 hours, checking from time to time and adding a little more boiling water if necessary.

5 Meanwhile, put the granulated sugar and wine in a pan and stir over a low heat until the sugar has dissolved. Increase the heat, bring to the boil and reduce the quantity of liquid by about half. Add the remaining berries and simmer until just cooked. Rub the fruit through a sieve to purée and remove the seeds.

6 Run a knife around the pudding and turn it out onto a warmed serving plate. Serve with the blackberry purée and cream, custard or ice cream.

Blackberry,
Port &
Almond Trifle

A stunning trifle with a moist, lemony-almondy cake soaked in dark blackberry and port jelly, then strewn with fresh blackberries and topped with a rich mascarpone cream. The cake can be made a couple of days in advance and the jelly is best made the day before you want to eat the trifle so that it can set. We find that making the trifle isn't very onerous because its various components can be fitted in whenever you have a spare moment. On the day of serving, it takes barely more than 5 minutes to whip up the mascarpone mixture and assemble the trifle.

Almond Cake:
125 g/4½ oz/generous ½ cup butter, softened, plus extra for greasing
125 g/4½ oz/generous ½ cup caster (superfine) sugar
2 large eggs
30 g/1 oz/3 tbsp plain (all-purpose) flour
125 g/4½ oz ground almonds
Zest and juice of 1 lemon

Jelly:
750 g/1 lb 10 oz blackberries
150 g/5½ oz/¾ cup granulated sugar
Juice of 1 lemon
6 leaves of gelatine
200 ml/7 fl oz port

To Assemble:
200 g/7 oz blackberries
500 g/1 lb 2 oz/generous 2 cups mascarpone cheese
75 ml/2½ fl oz/5 tbsp single (light) cream
75 g/2½ oz/⅓ cup caster (superfine) sugar
55 g/2 oz/½ cup flaked (slivered) almonds, toasted

1 Make the cake 2–3 days before you want to serve the trifle. Preheat the oven to 180°C/350°F/gas mark 4. Butter a 18 cm/7 inch diameter shallow cake tin and line with baking parchment.

2 Beat the butter and sugar together until pale and fluffy. Break in the eggs, one at a time, beating well after each egg and alternating with spoonfuls of flour. Gently stir in the ground almonds, the lemon zest and juice and scrape the mixture into the prepared tin.

3 Bake for about 25 minutes, until the top is firm to the touch and a skewer comes out clean. Leave to cool in the tin for 10 minutes and then turn out onto a wire rack. Once the cake is completely cold, wrap it in foil until you are ready to use it.

4 A day in advance, make the jelly. Put the blackberries in a saucepan with 100 ml/3½ fl oz/6–7 tbsp water and bring to the boil. Reduce the heat and simmer for 10 minutes until the berries are very soft. Squash them with a potato masher until they are completely crushed. Tip the mixture into a fine sieve and stir very gently to help it through, but don't press the flesh downwards through the sieve. Add the sugar and lemon juice to the blackberry juice and heat gently until the sugar has dissolved. Measure the juice: you should have around 600 ml/20 fl oz/ 2½ cups. If not, top it up with boiling water.

5 Soak the gelatine leaves in cold water for about 5 minutes to soften. Then squeeze out the excess water, one leaf at a time, and whisk into the hot blackberry juice until completely dissolved. Finally, add the port.

6 Unwrap the cake, break it into chunks and place in a glass trifle dish. Pour the jelly mixture over it, leave to cool and then chill in the fridge, preferably overnight.

7 To assemble the trifle, scatter the fresh blackberries over the cake and jelly in the trifle dish.

8 Whisk the mascarpone and cream together and then add the sugar until smooth and creamy, like softly whipped double (heavy) cream. Spread this over the blackberries, then scatter the toasted almonds over the top and serve.

Wild Raspberries

Probably the best of all wild fruits, raspberries are a native perennial of the British Isles and grow in hedgerows almost everywhere, though it is surely Scotland where they grow in greatest profusion. The fruit is the same as the cultivated raspberry, although smaller, and in fact there has been quite a bit of naturalization from cultivated strains. In any case, it is not hard to identify, although (luckily) many people seem to dismiss its ruby red fruits as unripe blackberries. Unfortunately, the fruit is much less generously distributed on the bushes than blackberries are, so they are harder work, though less scratchy.

When in Scotland in the summer, Ginny admits to obsessing about raspberries. She readily agrees to any golfing or fishing plans her husband proposes for himself (at which she would normally raise thousands of objections) so that she can go and have a good rummage along the hedges, with any children and dogs who might be willing. They were once rewarded with such abundance that she did not feel it profligate to make a raspberry crumble. It was absolutely delicious. Anyhow, wild raspberries do not keep well, so if you have more than you can eat raw, here are some recipes to tempt you.

Raspberry Vinegar

We know this sounds a bit 1980s, but raspberry vinegar does taste great and it is so useful in a raft of different dishes, both traditional and contemporary. Whisked with olive oil, thyme and maybe a touch of honey, it makes a divine dressing for a goat's cheese salad; use it to deglaze the pan after sautéing lamb or liver to give fruity depth to a sauce; or drizzle over vanilla ice cream for something refreshingly different. But raspberry vinegar's oldest and most celebrated use is as a cordial on a hot summer day. Pour it over ice and dilute 1 part vinegar with 5 parts lemonade or fizzy water.

900 g/2 lb raspberries
600 ml/20 fl oz/2½ cups cider vinegar
Approximately 450 g/1 lb/2¼ cups
granulated sugar

1 Put the raspberries in a glass or stainless steel bowl and mash them well. Pour over the vinegar and cover with clingfilm (plastic wrap) or a clean cloth. Leave for 5 days, stirring once or twice a day.

2 Tip the mixture into a jelly bag or a sieve lined with muslin (cheesecloth) and leave to drip into a large bowl for 2–3 hours, or until it has almost stopped dripping. Do not press or squeeze the raspberries or the vinegar will be cloudy. Clean and sterilize your bottles (see page 10).

3 Measure the liquid, then pour it into a stainless steel (not aluminium) saucepan. For every 600 ml/20 fl oz/2½ cups of the liquid, add 450 g/1 lb/2¼ cups sugar. Stir gently over a low heat until all the sugar has dissolved. Then increase the heat and boil gently for 10 minutes. Skim off any scum and leave to cool.

4 Using a funnel, pour into sterile bottles and store in a cool, dark place, where it will keep for a year.

*Makes about
1 litre/1¾ pints/
4 cups*

Wild Raspberry Jam

This is sooooo delicious, but don't try to make it too firm. Somehow the flavour is released more easily in a soft-set preserve.

1.2 kg/2 lb 10 oz raspberries
Juice of 2 lemons
1 kg/2¼ lb/5 cups granulated sugar

Makes 4–5 large jars

1 Put the raspberries, lemon juice and sugar into a heavy pan over a low heat, stirring occasionally, until the sugar has dissolved and the fruit is soft. Increase the heat and boil rapidly for 5–7 minutes, or until setting point is reached (see page 10). Ladle into warm, sterilized jars and seal.

Seedless Raspberry Jam

If you have a problem with the seeds and can't bear picking them out of your teeth, you could whizz the berries in a blender or food processor and then push the purée through a sieve or food mill, before making the jam in exactly the same way as above.

Vanilla Panna Cotta with Wild Raspberry Coulis

This is a wonderful, easy dessert, though it looks impressive and is very pretty. The only area where it is unforgiving is on the time front: you have to make the panna cotta the day before you want to eat it, or it may not set. You can team it with other kinds of sharp fruit, though in our experience some people are less enthusiastic about rhubarb or gooseberries. What a shame – more for us!

This panna cotta is somewhat lighter than you usually find in a restaurant, because we prefer it that way. However, if you like a creamier experience, replace the semi-skimmed milk with full-fat.

Panna Cotta:
6 leaves of gelatine
1 vanilla pod
600 ml/20 fl oz/2½ cups double (heavy) cream
600 ml/20 fl oz/2½ cups semi-skimmed (low-fat) milk
125 g/4½ oz/generous ½ cup caster (superfine) sugar

Raspberry coulis:
450 g/1 lb wild raspberries (frozen are OK, but let them thaw)
70 g/2½ oz/⅓ cup caster (superfine) sugar, or to taste

1 Soak the gelatine in cold water for about 5 minutes to soften.

2 Roll the vanilla pod between your fingers to loosen it, then split it lengthways and scrape out the seeds with a small flat knife. Put the seeds and pod into a saucepan and pour over the cream and milk. Add the sugar and bring the mixture slowly to the boil, stirring to dissolve the sugar. As soon as it comes to the boil, remove from the heat.

3 Squeeze out the excess water from the gelatine leaves, one leaf at a time, and add to the hot cream, beating after each addition to ensure the gelatine is dissolved and the vanilla seeds are evenly dispersed.

4 Strain through a sieve into a jug to remove the vanilla pod and any murky brown bits that have escaped from it. Then pour into 8 ramekins or individual pudding bowls. Cover with clingfilm (plastic wrap) and leave to cool, then put in the fridge overnight to set.

5 To make the coulis, whizz the raspberries in a blender or food processor and push the purée through a sieve to remove the seeds. Add sugar to taste and stir until it has dissolved.

6 To serve, hold each ramekin in a bowl of hot water for 5–10 seconds until the outside just melts. Invert onto a serving plate and drizzle round a pool of coulis.

Serves 8 (you can make half quantities if you want)

Serves 6

Cranachan

We have something of a tradition of holding Burns Night parties, and are always on the lookout for Scottish desserts. We had tried making cranachan a few times, but somehow it always disappointed. The toasted pinhead oatmeal was too austere and joyless, possibly even 'dour'. However, one of our friends told us about a cranachan-to-die-for he'd had, with flapjacky nuggets in it – and the pieces started to come together.

If you're pushed for time or feeling lazy, you could use a few handfuls of commercial, crunchy muesli in place of the homemade nuggets – but you would sacrifice the lovely honey/hazelnut flavour.

Crunchy Oat Nuggets:
40 g/1½ oz/3 tbsp butter
1 generous tbsp Scottish
 heather honey
55 g/2 oz/scant ¾ cup
 rolled oats
30 g/1 oz/2 tbsp soft brown
 sugar
30 g/1 oz/3 tbsp hazelnuts,
 roughly chopped
12 g/2 rounded tsp plain
 (all-purpose) flour

*Whisky Cream and
 Raspberry Mixture:*
600 ml/20 fl oz/2½ cups
 whipping cream
70 g/2½ oz/generous ½ cup icing
 (confectioners') sugar, sifted
5 tbsp Scotch whisky
500 g/1 lb wild raspberries
 (frozen will do, though fresh
 is best)
Caster (superfine) sugar

1 Preheat the oven to 180°C/350°F/gas mark 4. Line a baking sheet with baking parchment.

2 To make the oat nuggets, melt the butter and honey in a saucepan, then stir in the other ingredients until everything is well coated. Spread out on the lined baking sheet to a depth of about 5 mm/¼ inch (don't worry if it doesn't reach the edges) and bake for about 20 minutes, until golden brown. Leave to cool, then crumble into pieces and set aside. It can be stored in an airtight container for up to 3 days.

3 To make the whisky cream, whip the cream with the icing sugar and whisky until soft peaks form.

4 Divide the raspberries in half (preferably into pretty ones and ugly ducklings). Blitz the ducklings to make a purée, push through a sieve to remove the seeds and add caster sugar to taste.

5 Assemble the cranachan at the last minute. Layer the elements into six glasses, starting with raspberry purée and a few whole berries, then a layer of whisky cream, oat nuggets, cream, purée, berries, and finish with cream, nuggets and a few whole raspberries.

Wild Raspberry Bakewell

More a frangipane than a Bakewell really, but originally this was adapted from a Bakewell tart recipe, and the fresh raspberries ensure all the right flavours are present, although we think in a more delicious way. This is an absolutely dependable, standby pudding, which we have made successfully with all kinds of fruit, from gooseberries to greengages, bilberries to brambles, as well as raspberries. The crisp pastry is a perfect foil to the slightly gooey, caky, fruity filling. You can take it to friends' houses when an extra dessert is needed and it does not slop all over the car. It makes the most of a relatively small amount of fruit and we have not found anyone who has refused a slice, especially served warm with some ice cream. You can make a smaller tart if you want to, but we never do. Somehow, it always goes within 24 hours.

We don't like almond extract, so we haven't used it. However, if a Bakewell tart is unthinkable for you without almond extract, by all means add a few drops to the filling.

Shortcrust Pastry:
175 g/6 oz/1½ cups plain (all-purpose) flour
50 g/1¾ oz/4 tbsp cold butter, cubed
40 g/1½ oz/3 tbsp lard, cubed

Filling:
115 g/4 oz/½ cup butter, softened
115 g/4 oz/generous ½ cup caster (superfine) sugar, plus 1 tbsp
2 eggs
175 g/6 oz/generous 1¾ cups ground almonds
1 tsp baking powder
300 g/10½ oz raspberries
Icing (confectioners') sugar

1 Preheat the oven to 200°C/400°F/gas mark 6.

2 To make the pastry, rub together the flour, butter and lard, until it resembles fine breadcrumbs. (You can do this in a food processor, but it seems to turn out better if you do it by hand.) Add a little cold water, a tablespoon at a time, and stir with a knife until it just starts to come together into large crumbs. Try not to add too much water. If you do, you can rescue it by adding some more flour, but it won't be quite as good. Using your hands, form the pastry into a ball.

3 Roll out the pastry thinly and line a 28 cm/11 inch diameter tart dish or tin. Bend the pastry back over the side of the tin and cut it off with a slight overhang. Prick it all over with a fork and put it into the fridge for about 30 minutes (or freezer, if you're using a metal tin). We find that if we put a pricked, chilled pastry shell directly into the oven, it bakes beautifully and the sides stay upright – no need to line it with paper and dried beans. Bake the chilled tart for about 15 minutes, until lightly coloured. Leave to cool slightly. Reduce the oven temperature to 180°C/350°F/gas mark 4.

4 To make the filling, beat the butter and sugar together until light and fluffy. Beat in the eggs, one at a time, and if the mixture starts to curdle, add a spoonful of ground almonds and beat in. Mix the baking powder thoroughly into the remaining almonds and fold into the buttery mixture, using a metal spoon.

5 When the pastry is reasonably cool, spoon in the almond mixture. Scatter the raspberries on the top, leaving a little space between most of the berries, and press them lightly into the batter. Sprinkle over 1 tablespoon caster sugar. Return the tart to the oven and bake for 30–40 minutes, until the almond mixture is cooked but still a little sticky in the middle. Test by taking it out of the oven and pressing it near the centre. If you can hear lots of liquid-sounding bubbles bursting, it needs a few more minutes. Cover with foil if it starts to brown too darkly. Remove from the oven and dust with a little icing sugar. Serve warm if possible.

Bilberries

Superior in flavour to their imported North American cousin, the blueberry, bilberries are found patchily across the UK and northern Europe on windswept heaths, moors, open woodland and other acid soils. Yet, from July to September, most people pass right by, never seeing them, as the berries are small and grow close to the ground on low bushes. Identification is pretty simple: the berries look just like miniature versions of cultivated blueberries (see photographs pages 87 and 88).

You may know bilberries by another name: whortleberry, myrtle blueberry, huckleberry, whinberry, black-hearts and, in Ireland, fraughan – to name but a few. These names speak volumes about their popularity in times gone by, so why do we not see them on sale today? Well, apart from the fact they are extremely hard to cultivate, if you go out to pick them, you will probably understand the reason pretty quickly. Gathering bilberries is backbreaking work and it takes a long time to pick a relatively small quantity. The only exception we have ever personally encountered was in the far

north of Scotland, where Ginny found huge bilberries growing in such enormous quantity that she was able to generate the first – and so far only – bona fide bilberry glut we know about. And fabulous it was too! Anyhow, northern Scotland aside, we are rather glad that it is uneconomic to coll bilberries, as this makes a foraged haul so much more special.

In terms of how best to enjoy these tiny berries, there is a myriad of options. They are delicious just as they are, either straight off the bush or, if you are more patient, with cream and sugar back at home. If you only have a few, use them for decoration, or as a cheesecake topping. Bilberry jam is sublime, as not only is the fruit delicious, but it is relatively pipless. There are many Yorkshire recipes for bilberries, where for some reason 'mucky mouth pies' were a traditional feature of 'funeral teas', so we include a couple below. There are also many glorious European recipes, of which the French Tarte aux Myrtilles Sauvages is our favourite. Just love the thought of those savage myrtles!

Bilberry Jam

A few words of advice about bilberries and jam. Firstly, they don't contain much pectin, so you need to use lemon juice to boost it; you may also want to use jam sugar or commercial pectin to make sure. Secondly, unlike most other fruit, bilberries need to be properly cooked before you add the sugar, otherwise they can become a bit chewy.

1 kg/2¼ lb bilberries
Juice of 4 lemons
1 kg/2¼ lb/5 cups granulated sugar
  or jam sugar (with added pectin)

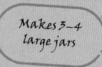

Makes 3–4 large jars

1 Put the bilberries, lemon juice and 150 ml/5 fl oz/ ²⁄₃ cup water in a heavy pan. Bring to the boil and simmer for about 10 minutes or until the berries are soft.

2 Add the sugar, turn the heat down to low and stir until all the sugar has dissolved. Then increase the heat and boil rapidly for 5–10 minutes, or until setting point is reached (see page 10). When the magic moment arrives, ladle the jam into warm, sterilized jars and seal.

Wild Blueberry Muffins

85 g/3 oz/6 tbsp butter
250 g/9 oz/2 cups plain
   (all-purpose) flour
2 tsp baking powder
Pinch of salt
150 g/5½ oz/¾ cup caster
   (superfine) sugar
300 ml/10 fl oz/1¼ cups buttermilk
   (or plain yogurt, or mix of yogurt
   and milk)
1 egg
150 g/5½ oz bilberries

Makes 8 large muffins (or 12 medium-sized ones)

These light muffins make a great brunch or afternoon tea when you return from a walk. They are quick and easy to make and slip down very easily with a cup of tea or coffee. They don't keep well, though, so either freeze unwanted muffins to be reheated on another day, or steel yourselves to finish them!

1 Preheat the oven to 180°C/350°F/gas mark 4. Line a muffin tin with paper muffin cases.

2 Melt the butter and let it cool slightly. Sift the flour, baking powder and salt into a large bowl and stir in the sugar. In a jug, mix together the buttermilk, egg and melted butter. Pour the wet ingredients into the dry and stir until just combined. Gently fold in the bilberries.

3 Spoon the batter into the muffin cases and bake for 25–30 minutes, until golden and firm. Transfer to a wire rack and eat while still slightly warm.

Bilberry Yorkshire Pudding

Yorkshire's answer to the classic French dish, clafoutis. A very light pudding, perfect to showcase your bilberry haul if it was quite meagre.

30 g/1 oz/2 tbsp butter, plus extra for greasing
1 egg
30 g/1 oz/2 tbsp caster (superfine) sugar, plus extra for dusting
1 tsp vanilla extract
30 g/1 oz/3 tbsp plain (all-purpose) flour
150 ml/5 fl oz/⅔ cup milk
115 g/4 oz bilberries

1 Preheat the oven to 200°C/400°F/gas mark 6. Generously butter a 4-hole Yorkshire pudding tin.

2 Melt the butter and let it cool slightly. In a bowl, whisk together the egg, sugar and vanilla. Whisk in the flour until smooth, then whisk in the milk and melted butter.

3 Put the Yorkshire pudding tin into the oven until the butter is sizzling hot. Pour the batter into the hot tin, scatter the bilberries on top of each pudding and return to the oven as quickly as possible. Bake for about 20 minutes, until risen and golden brown.

4 Sprinkle a little caster sugar over the puddings and return to the oven for 5 minutes. They will shrink back once removed from the oven (as you can see) but will still taste delicious. Serve immediately, with crème fraîche.

Serves 4

Individual Blaeberry Crumbles

This is a characteristically Yorkshire recipe, where mint was often combined with bilberries. (You can leave out the mint if you want, but we recommend it highly.) It would be more traditional to make a pie, but after you've spent all those hours on your hands and knees picking bilberries, we reckon you deserve a break!

We have chosen to make individual crumbles, because you may not (in fact, almost certainly will not) come home with a huge haul of berries. This recipe is easy to scale up or down. Also, if you are desperate to make this and don't have enough fruit, do consider adding some peaches or nectarines to the bilberries. They are not traditional, but the two fruits go well together, even with the mint.

400 g/14 oz bilberries
85 g/3 oz/scant ½ cup granulated sugar
2 tbsp lemon juice
4 tsp cornflour (cornstarch)
8 large fresh mint leaves, shredded

Crumble:
85 g/3 oz/scant ¾ cup plain (all-purpose) flour
55 g/2 oz/scant ¾ cup rolled oats
85 g/3 oz/scant ½ cup soft brown sugar
85 g/3 oz/6 tbsp butter

1 Preheat the oven to 180°C/350°F/gas mark 4.

2 Mix the bilberries with the sugar, lemon juice, cornflour and mint. Divide the mixture equally among four ramekins.

3 To make the crumble, mix together the flour, oats and sugar. Melt the butter in a saucepan, add the dry ingredients and mix thoroughly.

4 Top the berries with the crumble and put the ramekins on a baking sheet. Bake for 15–20 minutes, until the crumble is golden brown and the blueberries are bubbling. Leave to cool slightly, then serve with cream or custard.

Bilberry Tart

(Tarte aux Myrtilles Sauvages)

A recipe from the Vosges mountains in Alsace, France, where yummy bilberries hide in the bushes much like they do in the Lake District in England. This tart looks as wonderful as it tastes and shows off hard-won fruit to great advantage (although it must be said that it also works well with bought blueberries, fresh or frozen). The main issue to contend with is the bilberry juice, which can turn the pastry from crisp and delicious to sad and soggy. The flour and almond mixture helps to soak up the juices.

Depending on the size of your bilberry haul, you may need to use a smaller or larger tart tin. You can find the ideal size by tipping the berries into a tart tin (or tins): you want them to come a third of the way up the tin, when packed closely.

Pastry (pâte sablée):
85 g/3 oz/6 tbsp butter,
  softened
85 g/3 oz/scant ½ cup
  caster (superfine) sugar
175 g/6 oz/1½ cups plain
  (all-purpose) flour

Filling:
2 tbsp ground almonds
1 tbsp plain (all-purpose) flour
4 tbsp caster (superfine) sugar
350–400 g/12–14 oz bilberries
250 ml/9 fl oz/1 cup crème fraîche
4 egg yolks
Icing (confectioners') sugar for
  dusting

1 To make the pastry, beat the butter and sugar together, either in a food processor or by hand. Add the flour until the mixture resembles coarse crumbs. Add about 1 tablespoon cold water and quickly form into a dough. Shape into a ball with your hands, wrap in clingfilm (plastic wrap) and leave to rest in the fridge for at least 30 minutes.

2 Preheat the oven to 200°C/400°F/gas mark 6. You will need a tart tin about 24 cm/9½ inches in diameter.

3 Roll out the pastry on a floured surface or between two sheets of baking parchment, as thinly as you can. It is quite fragile and may break up, but don't despair, just put the pieces into the tin and stick them together with a little water. No one will see your patchwork in the finished tart. Prick the pastry all over with a fork. Put the tart tin in the freezer for 20 minutes. Bake blind (and if the pastry is semi-frozen you needn't faff about lining it with paper and dried beans, just put it straight into the oven) for about 15 minutes or until lightly coloured.

4 Reduce the oven temperature to 180°C/350°F/gas mark 4.

5 To make the filling, mix together the almonds, flour and 2 tablespoons of the caster sugar. When the pastry comes out of the oven, spread this mixture evenly over the pastry and spread the bilberries generously on top. Return to the oven for 10–15 minutes, to start the bilberries cooking.

6 Beat together the crème fraîche, egg yolks and remaining caster sugar and pour the mixture over the hot bilberries. Return to the oven for 15–20 minutes or until set. Turn off the oven and leave the tart for another 10 minutes before taking it out.

7 Leave to cool and serve at room temperature, dusted with icing sugar.

Elderberries

Both the flowers and the fruit of the elder bush are edible, though undoubtedly the flowers are the superior (see page 11). However, come late August, clusters of shiny black elderberries are plentiful and can be used to great advantage in some dishes. The berries are ripe when the stems turn red and the clusters begin to hang upside down (see photograph page 96). Do not be tempted to take unripe berries or those past their best, where the berries have started to wrinkle.

When picking elderberries, pick the whole cluster and take them home, where you can wash them and strip the juicy berries from the bitter (and poisonous) stalks with a fork and begin the labour of love of sorting the ripe black berries from the unripe green ones. Raw, the berries are mildly toxic, so they should always be cooked.

They have a sour and pleasantly fruity flavour but a few too many pips, so they are good added to other fruits – for example in a blackberry jelly or an apple pie – or as part of a mixed hedgerow jam (see page 100). There are a few dishes, however, where the use of elderberries cannot be surpassed. Elderberry wine was once so popular that whole orchards in Kent were planted for this purpose. In fact, elderberry was once so widely used to adulterate claret and port that in the mid-eighteenth century the cultivation of elder trees was forbidden in Portugal.

Elderberry Wine

This deep red, full-bodied wine is well worth the effort. Better still, it's practically free and once you've got the hang of it you can adapt it to your own taste. Feel free to experiment with adding other fruit. Adding an extra 1 kg/about 2 lb blackberries to the bucket with the elderberries makes an excellent port-style wine.

Use dark green wine bottles with corks or screw-top lids. Dark bottles will protect the colour of the wine from fading, though they will also stop you admiring it until you pour it out.

1.5 kg/3 lb 5 oz elderberries
1 kg/2¼ lb/5 cups granulated sugar
 – *for dry wine*
or 1.3 kg/3 lb/6½ cups granulated sugar
 – *for medium wine*
or 1.5 kg/3 lb 5 oz/7½ cups granulated sugar
 – *for sweet wine*
1.2 litres/2 pints/5 cups boiling water
1 sachet (1–2 tsp) of granulated red wine yeast
1 tsp yeast nutrient
1 tsp citric acid

Makes 6 x 75 cl bottles

1 Strip the elderberries from their stalks directly into a clean 5 litre/1 gallon/5 quart food-grade plastic bucket and crush them. Use a potato masher rather than your feet! Add the sugar and pour in the boiling water. Stir until the sugar has dissolved, then leave to cool to room temperature (approximately 21°C/70°F).

2 Once cool, add the yeast, yeast nutrient and citric acid. Cover and leave in a warm place to ferment vigorously for 4–5 days.

3 Strain through a sieve into a sterilized 5 litre/1 gallon/5 quart demijohn (glass or plastic), top up with cool, boiled water if necessary and fit a cork and airlock. Put the demijohn on a tray, in case the liquid bubbles over during the fermentation process, and leave in a dark place to continue to ferment gently for 4–6 weeks.

Note: It should not be left in a very cold place, or the fermentation will stop and may continue (explosively) later, once bottled. Once the fermentation has stopped, clean and sterilize the wine bottles. Siphon the wine into the bottles and label. Store for 3–6 months before you drink it.

Pontack Sauce

This sauce will give you a taste of really old English fayre. It was reputedly invented in the seventeenth century, in what was possibly London's first gastropub, the Pontack's Head Tavern, by Monsieur Pontac, its eponymous owner. It is a fruity, tart sauce with elderberries and spices, and it is great with liver, kidneys, duck, pork, or any rich meat. Allegedly, it is best after being kept for 7 years, but we've made a few amendments to the most authentic of recipes and we think it's fine to use immediately. In fact, we think that Jonathan Swift et al. might very well have preferred it.

Makes approximately 1 x 50 cl bottle

500 g/1lb 2 oz elderberries, washed and stripped from stalks
500 ml/18 fl oz/2 cups cider vinegar
400 g/14 oz/2 cups granulated sugar
200 g/7 oz shallots, sliced
6 cloves
4 allspice berries
1 blade of mace
40 black peppercorns
15 g/½ oz fresh root ginger, peeled and bruised

1 Put the elderberries and vinegar in a non-reactive casserole dish. Cover with the lid and put it into the oven at 100°C/212°F/less than gas mark ¼ as you go to bed.

2 The next morning, remove the casserole dish from the oven and replace it with the glass bottle or bottles you plan to use, to sterilize them.

3 Crush the berries in the vinegar with a potato masher and pour through a fine sieve to remove the pips. Return the juice to a saucepan and add the sugar, shallots and all the spices. Boil rapidly until reduced by about one-third. Strain the mixture again and pour it into the warm, sterilized bottle(s).

4 Store in a dark cupboard to protect its colour. You could keep some for 7 years to see if it matures and improves.

Elderberry Sorbet

700 g/1 lb 9 oz elderberries, washed and stripped from stalks
300 g/10½ oz/1½ cups granulated sugar
Juice of ½ lemon

Makes just under 1 litre/ 1³/₄ pints/4 cups

There is an especially good reason to make this ice if you have made some elderflower cordial earlier in the year, and that is to make a very elegant dish of elder*flower* sorbet (see page 20), accompanied by elder*berry* sorbet. If you haven't made the cordial, don't despair, you can always buy some – or just serve the lovely elderberry sorbet on its own.

1 Put the elderberries, sugar and 200 ml/7 fl oz/generous ¾ cup water in a pan over a low heat, stirring occasionally, until the sugar has dissolved. Simmer for a couple of minutes to ensure the elderberries are fully cooked. Whizz the mixture with a handheld blender and then push it through a fine sieve (very hard work) or a food mill on a fine setting to remove the pips. Add the lemon juice and leave the purée to cool completely.

2 When it is cold, tip the elderberry purée into an ice-cream maker and churn according to the manufacturer's instructions. Alternatively, to freeze without using an ice-cream maker, pour the mixture into a container and freeze, stirring briefly with a fork every 30 minutes to break up the ice crystals, until the sorbet is firm.

3 Store in a covered container in the freezer for up to 2 months.

Rowan Berries

The rowan or mountain ash tree is found throughout the British Isles. It is as much at home alone on a blasted heath as it is in our towns and cities, where it is often planted to be decorative. Its flowers are pretty, but unfortunately they smell very unpleasant. The attractive berries, which appear between August and November, are bright orange-red. Identification is simple while its ash-like leaves are in place, but since the berries are often picked in October, after the leaves have fallen, it can be more problematic. If you are going to pick the berries late, it's a good idea to make a positive identification in the summer. Fortunately, the only likely confusion is with the wild service or 'checkers' tree, which is not poisonous.

There are several 'issues' with rowan berries as a food item: they are sour, bitter, chock-full of pips and poisonous when raw. However, there is one, and only one, good reason to harvest them: rowan jelly. The best way to pick the berries is to snip the clusters whole from the tree, then strip them from the stalks once you get home.

Rowan Jelly

This jelly is a beautiful dark orange colour with a sharp and slightly bitter marmalade flavour. It perfectly complements lamb and is traditional with game.

Ginny and her mum once made jelly entirely from rowan berries, which was a total failure. They remember a highly unfavourable comment regarding ear wax... So do not make the mistake of thinking the apples are optional!

1 kg/2¼ lb rowan berries
1 kg/2¼ lb crab apples (or other tart apples)
Approximately 1 kg/2¼ lb/5 cups
  granulated sugar
Juice of 1 lemon

Makes 3–4 large jars

1 Set up a jelly bag or line a large sieve with muslin (cheesecloth) and place over a large bowl.

2 Wash the rowan berries and chop the crab apples roughly. Put the fruit into a heavy pan with 1.2 litres/2 pints/5 cups water and bring to the boil. Simmer until soft and pulpy. Tip the mixture into the jelly bag or muslin-lined sieve and leave to drip for at least 3–4 hours, ideally overnight.

3 Measure the juice into a pan. For every 600 ml/20 fl oz/2½ cups of juice, add 450 g/1 lb/2¼ cups sugar. Add the lemon juice and bring slowly to the boil, stirring until the sugar has dissolved. Boil rapidly for about 10 minutes before testing for set (see page 10). Pour the jelly into warm, sterilized jars and seal.

Berry Mixtures

It was impossible to know where to put these two recipes, so we gave up and decided to give them their own section. It's about using any wild fruit you can harvest and transforming it into something delicious to eat.

Hedgerow Jam or Jelly

The charm of this preserve is that it reflects a specific time and place. The fruits are what you happen to find on your ramble, so depending on what turns up, you may choose to turn the fruit into a jam, seedless jam or a jelly. For example, if you have mostly stony and pip-ridden fruit such as sloes and elderberries, we would recommend a jelly or seedless jam, whereas if you have large wild apples and damsons, you may prefer a straightforward jam. If the latter, it's best to core the apples and stone the plums. Many of the fruits may be low in pectin, so it's a good idea to ensure that a third to a half of your fruit is made up of pectin-rich apples, ideally tart, flavoursome crab apples. If you have mainly berries and plums, taste the mixture once you have added the sugar: you may wish to add the juice of one or two lemons to bring out the full fruity flavour. Hedgerow jam or jelly is delicious on toast and is a unique souvenir of a lovely autumn day.

2.5 kg/5½ lb mixed fruit, such as crab apples, sloes, damsons, blackberries and elderberries
2 kg/4½ lb/10 cups granulated sugar (for the jam, see below for the jelly)
115 g/4 oz/1 cup hazelnuts, finely chopped (optional in jam, but don't use in jelly)
Juice of 1 or 2 lemons (optional, see above)

Makes about 9–10 large jars of jam, or about half as many of jelly

To make jam:
1 Wash the fruit. Core the apples and chop them roughly, removing patches of really rough or badly blemished skin. Remove the stones from wild plums or damsons. Put all the fruit in a heavy pan with about 150 ml/5 fl oz/²⁄₃ cup water. Simmer gently until the apples have softened, and then add the sugar and hazelnuts, if using. Stir until the sugar has dissolved, then increase the heat and bring to the boil. Boil rapidly for about 10 minutes, until setting point is reached (see page 10). Pour into warm, sterilized jars and seal.

To make seedless jam or jelly:
1 Wash the fruit. Chop apples roughly, and put all the fruit into a heavy pan with 500 ml/18 fl oz/2¼ cups water. Bring to the boil and cook until soft and pulpy.

2 If making seedless jam, push the mixture through a sieve to get rid of pips and stones, or, even easier, put it through a food mill. Add the hazelnuts, if using, to the fruit purée.

3 If making jelly, put the mixture into a jelly bag or a sieve lined with muslin (cheesecloth) and leave it to drip into a bowl for 3–4 hours or overnight.

4 Measure the purée or juice and pour it back into the pan. For every litre/1¾ pints/4 cups of purée or juice, add 750 g/1 lb 10 oz/3¾ cups sugar. Put the pan over a low heat and stir until all the sugar has dissolved. Increase the heat and boil rapidly, without stirring, until setting point is reached (see page 10). Pour into warm, sterilized jars and seal.

Serves 6

Serendipity Summer Pudding

The best summer pudding we have ever eaten was made by Caro's mum, entirely from wild fruit, found by chance in a wood. Luckily, that particular wood was stuffed full of bilberries and raspberries. Yours will be different, as you will find your own serendipitous combination, but we're sure it will be just as delicious.

175 g/6 oz/generous ¾ cup granulated sugar
1.2 kg/2½ lb mixed wild berries, such as blackberries, bilberries, raspberries, elderberries or, possibly, wild plums, halved and stoned
7–8 slices day-old good-quality white bread, crusts removed

1 Put the sugar and 3 tbsp water into a large pan over a low heat, stirring occasionally, until the sugar has dissolved. Increase the heat and bring to the boil for 1 minute. Tip in the fruit and cook over a low heat for 3 minutes. The fruit will be softened but mostly intact. Put a sieve over a bowl and pour the fruit into the sieve to separate the fruit from the juice.

2 Line a 1.2 litre/2 pint/5 cup pudding bowl with clingfilm (plastic wrap), which will help you turn out the pudding. (We lost count of how many summer puddings disintegrated on us until we learned this trick.) Leave about 15 cm/6 inches of the clingfilm overhanging. Cut one slice of bread into a circle to fit the bottom of the pudding and then cut the rest in half, so that you have lots of rectangles.

3 Dip each piece of bread into the juice for a few seconds, starting with the circle for the bottom. Press each piece into the pudding bowl and stick the bread rectangles together by overlapping them slightly – more at the bottom than the top. Spoon in the softened fruit to just below the lip of the bowl. Dip the remaining bread in the juice and place on top. Trim off any overhang with scissors. Put the leftover juice in a jug and keep it in the fridge for later.

4 Bring the clingfilm loosely up and over the top of the pudding. Put a close-fitting plate on top of the pudding and weigh it down with cans. Chill for 6 hours, or overnight.

5 To serve, open out the clingfilm, invert the pudding onto a pretty plate and remove the clingfilm. Serve with a jug of the juice and another of thick pouring cream. The cream really is an essential part of this pudding, so don't omit it!

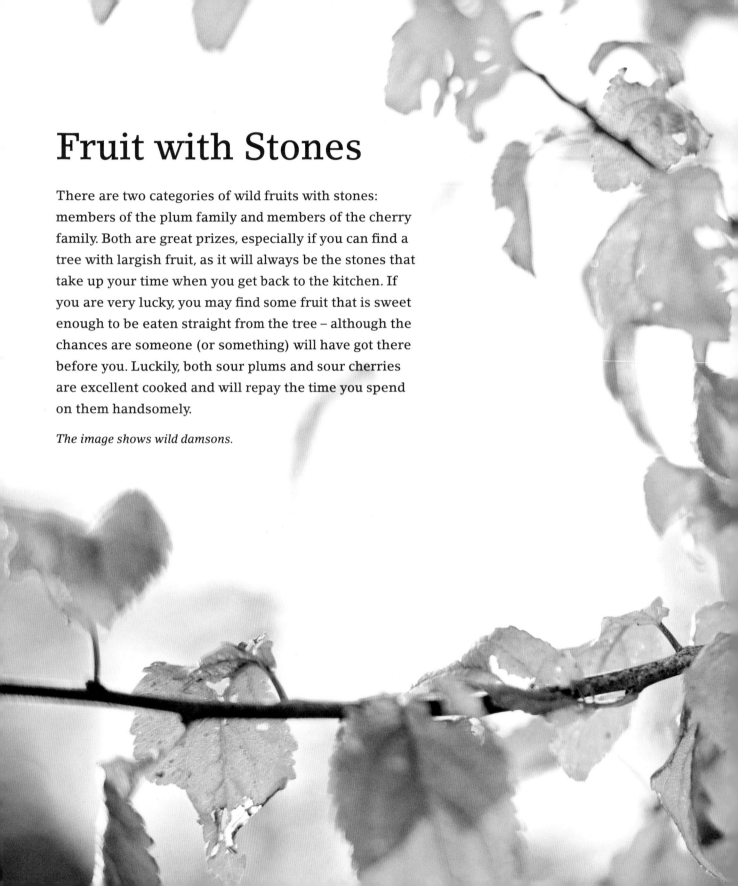

Fruit with Stones

There are two categories of wild fruits with stones: members of the plum family and members of the cherry family. Both are great prizes, especially if you can find a tree with largish fruit, as it will always be the stones that take up your time when you get back to the kitchen. If you are very lucky, you may find some fruit that is sweet enough to be eaten straight from the tree – although the chances are someone (or something) will have got there before you. Luckily, both sour plums and sour cherries are excellent cooked and will repay the time you spend on them handsomely.

The image shows wild damsons.

Wild Cherries

The small- to medium-sized trees are found throughout the British Isles, more commonly at the edge of woods than in hedgerows and, like the native rose, are often used as municipal planting. The wild cherry tree's billowing white blossom heralds spring like no other and, down the ages, has made poets swoon and country folk make merry. The cherry is the fruit of perfection, of heaven. Bunches of cherries used to be dangled flirtatiously by young women to entice their man.

The true wild cherry fruit is smaller than the cultivated varieties and much more sour; use it in all the same recipes but add extra sugar to make up for its tartness. Often cherry trees that are growing in the wild are wildings, the product of stones discarded from cultivated fruit. We don't think it really matters.

Harvesting the cherries, in late June and July, is the difficult part: as soon as the fruits start to ripen, the tree will be under siege from the birds. You will need to pick the fruit slightly underripe and let it ripen at home if you want any chance of a decent crop.

Wild Cherries in Brandy

Because it's nigh-on impossible to buy sour cherries in Britain, cherries in brandy are a treat that really can only be enjoyed by those of us who collect wild cherries, or by the lucky few who have a sour cherry tree in the garden. We like them best with very good vanilla ice cream or with an indulgent chocolate mousse. Put a small amount of the brandy syrup in the bottom of a glass and top up with sparkling white wine to create a lovely wild cherry cocktail.

500 g/1 lb 2 oz wild or other sour cherries, with or without their stems
300 g/10½ oz/1½ cups granulated sugar
About 300 ml/10 fl oz/1¼ cups brandy (we use inexpensive supermarket own-label brandy)

Makes about 850 ml/1½ pints/3½ cups (depending on the size of your cherries and how closely they pack.)

1 Sterilize one or more wide-mouthed bottling jars (see page 10).

2 Wash the cherries and dry them thoroughly. Decide whether you want to keep the stems on the cherries: they can look very pretty left on, if you intend to use them decoratively. Pack the fruit as closely as possible into the jar(s), sprinkling the sugar generously between each layer.

3 When you reach the top of the jar and have used all the sugar, fill it with brandy, ensuring you cover all the cherries. Tilt the jar to get rid of any air bubbles, then seal. Put it in a dark cupboard, to keep the colour bright, but do not put it out of mind, as you need to tip the jar upside down every day for a week, or until all the white sugar has disappeared.

4 After this, it can be left to macerate. Do not open the jar until it has been sitting quietly for a full month. Alternatively, you can leave it until Christmas and then dress it up in ribbons as a fabulous gift.

Sour Cherry Jam

This fabulously red jam is wonderful on toast and also has a special affinity with chocolate. We remember the original and delicious Black Forest gateau before its name became tarnished by various frozen abominations. Try sandwiching a chocolate sponge cake with cherry jam, or adding a little to your chocolate cupcake ingredients before you cook them. Intriguingly grown-up and somehow more-ish!

1.5 kg/3 lb 5 oz pitted cherries
1.5 kg/3 lb 5 oz granulated sugar
Juice of 1 lemon

Makes 4–5 large jars

1 Put the cherries in a saucepan with just enough water to come two-thirds of the way up the pan. Add the sugar and lemon juice and heat gently, stirring occasionally, until all the sugar has dissolved. Increase the heat and boil rapidly until setting point is reached (see page 10). Pour into warm, sterilized jars and seal immediately.

Wild Cherry Clafoutis

Caro spent her teenage years living in the south of France, where she was taken under the wing of a retired English teacher. Madame Bosseaux taught her French but just as importantly introduced her to the wonders of many classic French dishes, delighted to have such a greedy and open-minded pupil! Clafoutis is basically a Yorkshire pudding with fruit, traditionally sour cherries, and is as light and delicious as you could imagine. In the UK it is pretty much impossible to buy sour cherries – you need to find them wild or grow them – which is probably why this dish is not known so well here. We have found, though, that sweet cherries also work well. The French don't pit their cherries when making this, but if yours are large enough, we feel the extra step, although fiddly, is very well worth it.

500 g/1 lb 2 oz cherries, pitted if
  you like
70 g/2½ oz plain (all-purpose) flour
½ tsp salt
55 g/2 oz/¼ cup granulated sugar,
  plus 2 tbsp for sprinkling
4 eggs
175 ml/6 fl oz/¾ cup milk
60 g/2¼ oz/4½ tbsp butter

1 If you like, pit the cherries (you'll need a cherry stoner). Preheat the oven to 200°C/400°F/gas mark 6.

2 Put the flour and salt into a bowl and add 55 g/2 oz/¼ cup sugar. Make a well in the centre and whisk in the eggs, one by one. When you have a smooth batter, whisk in the milk. In a small saucepan, heat 40 g/1½ oz/3 tbsp of the butter until it is foaming and has started to go slightly brown. Stir the hot, nutty butter and cherries into the batter.

3 Put the remaining butter in a 24 cm/9½ inch diameter ceramic tart dish and place in the oven until it is melted and foaming. Remove the dish from the oven, swirl the butter all round and sprinkle 1 tablespoon sugar over the butter. Pour in the batter and bake for about 30 minutes, until puffed up and golden brown. Remove from the oven, sprinkle with the remaining tablespoon of sugar and pop it back into the oven for about 5 minutes to form a delicious crust. The clafoutis will sink back somewhat as it comes out of the oven, but don't worry. Serve warm, with crème fraîche or good vanilla ice cream.

Wild Plums,
Bullaces, Damsons
& Cherry Plums

There is a lot of confusion over definitions here: are wild plums really wild, or are they escaped cultivated plums? Are damsons just domesticated bullaces? And what on earth are cherry plums? In truth, there seems to have been a great deal of genetic intermingling and we don't think it matters a jot. The point is, whether it's yellow, red, green, purple or blue, small, medium or large, if it looks like a plum, has a stone in the middle of it, and tastes like a plum, it is indeed a plum of sorts, and you can use it in all manner of delicious foods.

Cherry plums tend to ripen early, about July, while other wild plums, damsons and bullaces can be ripe from August through to October.

Besides varying greatly in size, plums come in a spectrum of flavours, from sour to sweet-with-just-a-tinge-of-sourness, so you will need to taste any you find and make up your mind about how to use them. You may be able to eat them just as they are, or they may need to be lightly poached and used in crumbles, cakes, tarts or pies, or they may perhaps benefit from the greater amount of processing (and stone removal) needed to make a cheese or a chutney.

Wild Plum Jam with Almonds

1.5 kg/3 lb 5 oz wild plums
1.2 kg/2 lb 10 oz/6 cups granulated sugar
Juice of 1 lemon
About 20 plum stones, cracked open
 (optional, see above)
150 g/5½ oz/1½ cups flaked (slivered)
 almonds (optional)

Makes 5–6 large jars

You can use any kind of plums, damsons or bullaces for this, though the level of tartness/ripeness will affect the flavour. We both like a jam with a good amount of acidity.

Extracting the stones from the fruit is the major issue, as your methodology will affect the final texture of the jam. To achieve a jam with discernible fruit pieces, you need to cut the plums in halves (or quarters if they are very large) and remove the stones before you start cooking. If your plums are particularly small or the stones are welded strongly to the flesh, this will be next to impossible. It is allegedly possible to slit the plums with a knife, thereby aiding the escape of the stones during cooking as the plums collapse. You can try this if you want to. We have, and it was a total nightmare, with the plum stones stubbornly remaining inside the plums.

The real alternatives are to give up altogether on stone removal and go for a more rustic form of jam, which will have the benefit of allowing your family to play 'Tinker, Tailor, Soldier, Sailor' at breakfast with the stones they pick off their toast. (If you do this, we advise leaving out the almonds, as it could all get a bit confusing.) OR you can cook the plums with just the water until they become soft, and then put them through a food mill, which will remove the stones and reduce the fruit to a purée. Return the purée to the pan and proceed with the sugar and lemon juice. You will lose the discernible pieces of fruit, but the magnificent flavour is retained, and the flaked almonds do give the jam texture.

1 Wash the plums and put them into a heavy-bottomed pan with the sugar, lemon juice and 200 ml/7 fl oz/generous ¾ cup water. Heat gently, stirring occasionally, until the sugar has dissolved. Meanwhile, tie up the cracked plum stones and kernels in muslin (if using) and add them to the pot. When all the sugar has dissolved, bring the mixture to the boil and keep it at a rolling boil for about 10 minutes, or until setting point is reached (see page 10).

2 Remove the pan from the heat. Add the almonds, if using, and stir them in gently. If they rise to the top, leave the jam to cool for 10–15 minutes, stirring occasionally to stop a skin from forming. When the almonds remain suspended in the jam, it is ready to be filled into warm, sterilized jars. Seal immediately.

Damson Jelly & Damson Cheese

1.5 kg/3 lb 5 oz damsons
1.2 kg/2 lb 10 oz/6 cups
  granulated sugar
Juice and flesh of 1 lemon
Glycerine (optional)

Two lovely preserves for you to try. Your choice might depend on the abundance of damsons (jelly will make less), on how energetic you feel (cheese is harder work) or how much time you have (jelly takes longer). Both dispense with the stoning problem one has with jam, and both are very good, their sharp fruitiness making them superb accompaniments to creamy cheeses such as Camembert, and to rich meats such as shoulder of lamb or pork belly. They are also good on toast and in pastries, particularly chocolate ones.

In case you're wondering, a fruit cheese has nothing to do with dairy ingredients. 'Cheese' is the old English term for a smooth-textured fruit preserve. It may refer to the fact they are traditionally made to be quite firm, and they can be turned out onto your cheeseboard and sliced, rather than spooned. If you want to do this, put the hot preserve into straight-sided jars or small bowls – ideally brushed with glycerine – or else you'll never get it out.

1 Wash the damsons and put them into a heavy-bottomed pan with 200 ml/7 fl oz/generous ¾ cup water. Bring to the boil and simmer for about 10 minutes, until the damsons are soft and collapsing. Now you have to choose: jelly or cheese?

2 To make jelly, tip the mixture into a jelly bag or a large sieve lined with muslin (cheesecloth) and leave to drip for at least 4 hours, preferably overnight. Do not squeeze, or your jelly will be cloudy. Pick out about 25 stones from the strained pulp and throw the rest away.

3 To make cheese, either push the damson mush through a sturdy sieve, until only the stones and some of the skins are left behind. If you have a food mill, you will have a much easier time of it, as you can process the fruit pulp through that on the medium setting. Save about 25 stones.

4 Put the stones in a tea towel and bash them with a hammer until they crack open. Tie the crumbly mess of stones and kernels into a piece of muslin and make sure it is secure. You don't want any bits escaping into the fruit, you just want to harvest the pectin from the stones.

5 Add the juice or purée to your heavy-bottomed pan with the sugar, lemon juice and bag of stones. Heat gently, stirring, until all the sugar has dissolved. Then bring the mixture to the boil and keep it at a rolling boil for 15–20 minutes, stirring frequently to prevent it from catching, before testing for set (see page 10). If it is not ready, keep testing every 5 minutes. If you want to be able to turn out your cheese, it needs to be quite firmly set: when you put a drop on a cold plate it should stay in a mound, with no liquid running off.

6 Ladle the preserve into warm, sterilized jars and seal immediately. If you are planning to turn your cheese out, use straight-sided jars, and brush a little glycerine inside each jar before filling.

Pickled Plums

These beauties are a kind of Chinese-y pickle, great with barbecued meat or roast duck or as a really different accompaniment for cheese or cold meats. Although it may seem a lot of sugar, the plums still retain their sharpness, so we would advise you not to reduce the amount you add until you've tried it once.

Makes two 500 ml/18 fl oz/ 2 cup Kilner-type jars, or 4–5 large jam jars

300 ml/10 fl oz/1¼ cups cider vinegar
500 g/1 lb 2 oz/2½ cups granulated sugar
4 cardamom pods, lightly crushed
6 black peppercorns
2 small cinnamon sticks
1 star anise
½ tsp salt
2 fresh medium-hot chillies
1 kg/2¼ lb wild plums, washed and thoroughly dried

1 Bring the vinegar, sugar and spices – but not the chillies – slowly to the boil, stirring until the sugar has dissolved. Add the chillies and boil the mixture fiercely until it becomes thicker and syrupy. Leave it to cool completely.

2 Meanwhile, sterilize your jars and lids (see page 10). How you deal with your plums and their stones will depend on their size. If they are large and it is relatively easy to part them from their stones, cut them in half and de-stone. If not, prick each plum with something sharp and leave the stones in. Remember to warn your guests when serving.

3 Tuck one chilli down the side of two of the jars and pack the plums in as tightly as you can. Pour over the cold pickling liquid and spices to within 1 cm/½ inch of the top of the jar. Put the lids on and store them in a cool, dark place for at least a month, tipping them upside down about once a week. Once opened, keep in the fridge and eat within a couple of weeks.

Bullace Chutney

Makes 5–6 large jars

This can be made with any kind of wild plum or damson. The main difference will be in the colour: bullaces make it a gorgeous shade of beetroot. Chopped apples, vegetables and raisins provide the texture in this chutney. We use a food processor and aim for about 5 mm/¼ inch dice for the apples, carrots and onions. It is good in a cheese or ham sandwich.

1 kg/2¼ lb wild plums
300 g/10½ oz/1½ cups demerara sugar
350 ml/12 fl oz/scant 1½ cups cider vinegar
400 g/14 oz onions, chopped
400 g/14 oz dessert apples, cored and chopped (not peeled)
200 g/7 oz carrots, chopped (not peeled)
115 g/4 oz/scant ¾ cup raisins
3 garlic cloves, crushed
40 g/1½ oz peeled fresh ginger, grated
1 tsp ground ginger
1 tsp ground allspice
1 tsp dried crushed chilli
1 tsp salt

1 Put the plums in a pan with a very small quantity of water and bring them to the boil. Simmer for about 10 minutes or until the plums are collapsing. Either process the plum mush through a food mill, or push it through a sieve, to get rid of the stones.

2 Put the plum purée in a heavy-bottomed pan and add all the remaining ingredients. Heat gently, stirring occasionally, until all the sugar has dissolved. Increase the heat and bring to the boil, stirring regularly to prevent anything burning on the bottom. Keep boiling, to evaporate the water and vinegar, until a wooden spoon, scraped quickly across the bottom, reveals a fleeting, silvery glimpse of the pan. This means the chutney is thick enough to be bottled.

3 Ladle the chutney into warm, sterilized jars and put on the lids before it cools. This chutney is ready to be eaten immediately, though it will keep unopened for a couple of years.

Slow-Roasted Pork with Damsons

This is a super-easy, super-delicious dinner for six. Pork belly is our favourite cut of pork, as its fattiness gives it a melting texture and superb flavour. Add a layer of crunchy, salty, aniseedy crackling and a splash of plummy acid-sweetness, and we are transported to heaven! Ask your butcher to score the rind of the pork well.

1.5 kg/3 lb 5 oz piece of pork belly
2 tsp fennel seeds, crushed in a pestle and mortar, plus extra for the plum sauce
Salt and pepper
750 g/1 lb 10 oz damsons or wild plums
300 ml/10 fl oz/1¼ cups dry white wine
1 tbsp granulated sugar, or to taste

1 Remove the pork from the fridge and uncover it an hour before you want to start cooking, to allow it to come to room temperature. Preheat the oven to 230°C/450°F/gas mark 8.

2 Dry the pork thoroughly with paper towels. Rub the crushed fennel seeds and a good sprinkling of salt into the rind, pushing them into the scored fat. Put the meat in a roasting pan and then into the hot oven, to give it a good sizzle and start the crackling off.

3 After 30 minutes, turn the oven temperature down to 140°C/275°F/gas mark 1 and cook the pork for a further 2 hours.

4 After 1 hour, put the plums into an ovenproof dish, pour over the wine and sprinkle in the sugar. Put the dish, uncovered, into the oven for an hour.

5 Check that the pork is meltingly soft: it may need a further 30 minutes in the oven. But assuming it is cooked to perfection, leave it in a warm place to rest, covered with foil.

6 Meanwhile, finish off the plum sauce. Pick through the damsons with a small spoon, taking out the stones. Put the damsons into a saucepan, break them up a bit by stirring with a fork, and bring to the boil. Adjust the sweetness to taste and add a few crushed fennel seeds, if liked. Add salt and pepper to taste and keep warm until needed.

7 Slice the pork and serve with a pool of plum sauce, mashed potatoes and green vegetables.

Wild Plum and Pistachio Cake

You can make this cake with any of the plum family, or indeed with cherries – if you can face stoning them. In case you are wondering where the plums are in the cake opposite, we made it with greeny-yellow ones. It is very light and fruity and is probably at its very best about an hour after it comes out of the oven, still slightly warm and very moist. It is perfectly partnered with crème fraîche or vanilla ice cream. It is equally good made with almonds, but the colour is not quite so interesting. And if you have fussy kids, don't worry, they won't be able to tell it's got nuts in it until you tell them – after they've finished their second helping!

500 g/1 lb 2 oz wild plums
175 g/6 oz/¾ cup unsalted butter, softened, plus extra for greasing
175 g/6 oz/generous ¾ cup caster (superfine) sugar, plus extra for sprinkling
Grated zest and juice of 1 lemon
3 large eggs
100 g/3½ oz/generous ¾ cup unsalted pistachio nuts, ground
100 g/3½ oz/generous ¾ cup self-raising flour, sifted
Icing (confectioners') sugar, for dusting

1 Preheat the oven to 170°C/325°F/gas mark 3. Butter a 20 cm/8 inch springform tin and line the bottom with baking parchment. Halve the plums and remove the stones.

2 Cream the softened butter, caster sugar, lemon zest and juice until pale and fluffy, using an electric mixer. Beat in the eggs one at a time, alternating with a spoonful of the ground nuts. Add the remaining nuts and continue to whisk until you are confident you have maxed out on airy fluffiness. Lightly fold in the sifted flour. Spoon half the mixture into the prepared cake tin. Cover with half the plums, then cover them with the remaining cake mixture. Smooth out the top and finish with a layer of plum halves, cut side uppermost (which will look fabulous if they don't sink!). Sprinkle with a little more sugar.

3 Bake for about 1 hour, but check after 30 minutes and cover with foil if the cake is browning too much. The cake is done when it is golden and firm to the touch and a skewer comes out reasonably cleanly. Leave to cool in the tin for 10 minutes and then transfer to a wire rack to cool completely. Dust with icing sugar just before serving.

Wild Plum
Ice Cream

Wild plums and bullaces make much better ice creams than their cultivated cousins because they tend to have a stronger flavour and more acidity; as they are often an intense purple colour, they produce a very pretty pink ice cream. We like to serve this with very thin almond biscuits.

400g/14 oz wild plums
200 g/7 oz/1 cup caster (superfine) sugar, or to taste
200 ml/7 fl oz/generous ¾ cup single (light) cream – or double (heavy) cream, if you don't have an ice-cream maker
200 g/7 oz/generous ¾ cup plain yogurt
1 tsp vanilla extract

Makes about
1 litre/1¾ pints/
4 cups

1 Heat the plums in a pan with 3 tablespoons water. Bring to the boil and then simmer gently until the plums are soft. Rub them through a sieve or put them through a food mill to remove the stones. Add the sugar to the warm plum purée and stir until dissolved. Taste to ensure it is sweet enough, bearing in mind that plums vary in acidity and also that cold numbs the sensation of sweetness. You may need to add a little more sugar. Leave the plum mixture to cool, then chill in the fridge.

2 If you have an ice-cream maker, add the single cream, yogurt and vanilla to the plum mixture and churn according to the manufacturer's instructions. Scoop it into a 1 litre/1¾ pint/4 cup capacity container, cover and store in the freezer for up to 2 months.

3 If you don't have an ice-cream maker, use double cream and whip it before mixing with the plum purée and yogurt. This will ensure you get more air in the mixture and stop it freezing too hard. Pour the mixture into a container and freeze, stirring briefly with a fork every 30 minutes to break up the ice crystals, until frozen.

4 Remove the ice cream from the freezer about 15–20 minutes before you want to serve it.

5 The ice cream will keep in a covered container in the freezer for up to 2 months.

Serves 6

Damson Fool with Chocolate Thins

Fools are wonderfully simple to prepare and really showcase the flavour of the fruit. Damsons are ideal because their tartness is beautifully offset by the rich cream. The thin chocolate biscuits are dark and intense. They will keep in an airtight container for up to 5 days and so can usefully be made in advance.

Damson Fool:
500 g/1 lb 2 oz damsons, halved and stoned
85 g/3 oz caster (superfine) sugar
300 ml/10 fl oz/1¼ cups double (heavy) cream

Chocolate Thins:
140 g/5 oz/generous ½ cup unsalted butter, softened
100 g/3½ oz/½ cup caster (superfine) sugar
60 g/2¼ oz good-quality milk chocolate, melted
140 g/5 oz/generous 1 cup plain (all-purpose) flour
60 g/2¼ oz unsweetened cocoa powder

1 To make the fool, put the damsons in a pan with 2 tablespoons water and simmer gently until they are soft. Stir in the sugar, whizz the lot in a food processor and leave to cool. Whip the cream until soft peaks form and then fold it into the damson mixture. Pour into six glasses or glass serving bowls and put in the fridge to set.

2 To make the chocolate thins, clean out the food processor and whizz the butter and sugar until pale and fluffy. Add the melted chocolate, followed by the flour and cocoa powder and process until the dough comes together. Wrap in clingfilm (plastic wrap) and put in the fridge for 30 minutes.

3 Heat the oven to 190°C/375°F/gas mark 5. Line a baking sheet with baking parchment or non-stick liner.

4 Roll out the dough between two pieces of baking parchment to approximately 5 mm/¼ inch thick. Use a small round cutter to stamp out the dough: you should be able to make about 12–15 rounds. Place them on the lined baking sheet and bake for about 7 minutes, but check after 5 minutes for any signs of darkening around the edges. Transfer to a wire rack to cool.

5 Serve the damson fool with a plate of chocolate thins.

Damson & Apple Eve's Pudding

Eve's pudding, so simple and yet so scrumptious, has fallen out of favour and you will be hard pressed to find a recipe for it in a cookery book today. Luckily Ginny's mum is a cook in the traditional vein and we have been able to enjoy her full repertoire of classic British puddings since we were children. It is basically fruit with sponge cake on top, and is usually made with apples but can be made with any fruit of which you have a glut. Damsons and dessert apples together are a great combination because the apple tames the intense sourness of the damsons (as well as reducing the number of stones you have to spit out), while the damsons add their pink juiciness. We like it best when the fruit is *just* cooked and the sponge mixture is *not quite fully* cooked and you get a gloriously gooey coming together of juice and cake in the middle.

Fruit Mixture:
About 300 g/10½ oz damsons
About 300 g/10½ oz dessert apples, peeled, cored and chopped into damson-sized pieces
75 g/2¾ oz/⅓ cup granulated sugar

Sponge Topping:
55 g/2 oz/¼ cup soft margarine or butter, softened, plus extra for greasing
55 g/2 oz/¼ cup caster (superfine) sugar
1 egg
55 g/2 oz/½ cup self-raising flour
¼ tsp baking powder
1 tsp vanilla extract
Handful of flaked (slivered) almonds (optional)

1 Preheat the oven to 180°C/350°F/gas mark 4. Butter an ovenproof baking dish about 18 cm/7 inches in diameter.

2 Put the whole damsons, chopped apples and granulated sugar in the baking dish. It should look pretty deeply filled, as the fruit will collapse as it cooks. Try to level the surface, so the sponge mixture stays mainly on the top.

3 Put the margarine or butter, caster sugar, egg, flour, baking powder and vanilla into a food processor or mixing bowl and pulse or mix until evenly combined and smooth. Spread it as evenly as possible over the fruit, covering all the fruit. Scatter the flaked almonds over the top, if using. Bake for 45–50 minutes, until golden and the sponge springs back when pushed gently. Leave to cool slightly before serving. Serve warm, with thick custard, cream, or good vanilla ice cream.

Sloes or Blackthorn

The most common form of wild plum, and possibly the ancestor of all plums, sloes are found throughout the British Isles, though they are less abundant in the north of Scotland. The fruits appear in September and can often be picked through to November. They are characteristically dusty blue and quite beautiful, though they are guarded well by long spikes or 'blackthorns' (see photograph page 129). They are also the most powerfully astringent fruit, which are eaten raw really only as childhood dares. However, this does mean they are excellent in cordials, gin and jellies, which benefit from their strong flavour.

Sloe & Apple Jelly

This really conjures up childhood for us. Being able to create something beautiful and delicious from the fruit of a few scratchy bushes and some manky-looking windfall apples was nothing less than miraculous. And even today, we love this tart, characterful preserve. As with most jellies, it is truly versatile: great on toast, superb with rich meats like duck or lamb, and a star turn when melted with a few drops of water and used as a glaze on a smart fruit tart. The apples are not optional. Without them, the jelly will be way too sour.

500 g/1 lb 2 oz sloes
1 kg/2¼ lb crab apples or windfall apples, not peeled or cored, but bruises removed and chopped
Granulated sugar

Makes 4 large jars

1 Tip all the sloes and chopped apples into a large, heavy-bottomed pan. Add water to come halfway up the fruit. Bring to the boil and simmer until the apples are pulpy and the sloes have revealed their stones. Tip the mixture into a jelly bag or a sieve lined with muslin (cheesecloth). Leave to drip into a large bowl for 12 hours or overnight.

2 Measure the juice before putting it back into the cleaned pan. For every 500 ml/18 fl oz/2 cups of juice, add 500 g/1 lb 2 oz/2½ cups sugar. Stir over a low heat until all the sugar has dissolved. Then increase the heat and boil, without stirring, until setting point is reached (see page 10).

3 Ladle the jelly into warm, sterilized jars and seal. Store in a cool, dark place to preserve the colour.

Sloe Cordial

Makes 2 x
75cl bottles

2 kg/4½ lb sloes
Juice of 2 lemons, strained
Granulated sugar

This cordial is like an intensely plummy, slightly less sweet version of Ribena (blackcurrant cordial), seen here on the left, with Crab Apple Cordial on the right (see page 137). It is enjoyed by children and adults alike, though we think the very best use for it is in the bottom of a glass of sparkling wine, to make a fabulous, celebratory kind of sparkling 'Kir Anglaise'. It is also great on ice cream or in apple crumbles, not just for its flavour, but also for its lovely pink colour. If you feel you might want to moderate the astringency of the sloes, you can mix them 50:50 with crab (or other) apples, for a slightly mellower cordial.

1 Wash the sloes and put them in a large, heavy-bottomed pan with 1 litre/1¾ pints/4 cups water. Bring to the boil and simmer for about 15 minutes, or until the sloes are mushy. Tip the mixture into a very fine jelly bag or a large sieve lined with muslin (cheesecloth). Leave to drip into a large bowl for about 4 hours or overnight. Do not press it through.

2 When the juice has finished dripping through, add the lemon juice to the sloe juice and measure it before returning it to the pan. For every 100 ml/3½ fl oz/6–7 tbsp of juice, add 90 g/3¼ oz/scant ½ cup sugar. Bring it slowly to a rolling boil, stirring to dissolve the sugar. Skim off any scum and remove from the heat. Taste to check it is sweet enough; you may need to add more sugar.

3 Pour through a funnel into warm, sterilized glass bottles and seal. Keep in the fridge and use within a month or two. Alternatively, pour into plastic bottles and freeze. If you would like to keep it for up to a year, follow the water bath sterilization method (see page 11).

4 To serve, dilute with water approximately in the ratio of 1:5. Top with ice and a sprig of fresh mint.

Sloe Gin
(or Vodka)

800 g/1 lb 12 oz sloes
280 g/10 oz/scant 1½ cups
   granulated sugar
1 bottle (700 ml) gin, at least
   40% abv

*Makes
1 litre/
1¾ pints/
4 cups*

Oh, my! What a fantastic thing this is. We have been making sloe gin as Christmas presents for years, but now it is getting seriously trendy, spawning dozens of cocktails as well as recipes for sauces and other good things. The best news is that it's incredibly easy to make, and requires no specialist kit. On the flip side, it takes quite a long time and stains your fingers (and anything else it comes into contact with) evilly. Still, it's worth it.

If you prefer, substitute vodka for gin (or indeed damsons for sloes).

There is a lot of chat on the internet about how it's best to pick sloes after the first frosts have 'bletted' them – in other words, turned them a bit rotten and squishy. We cannot comment, except to say that we have always made sloe gin with pristine, fresh, firm sloes picked in September/early October in the late summer sunshine – and the result has been gorgeous. We do not feel the need to experiment further.

Before you go picking, make sure you have some big bottles with screw caps or swing tops that you can sterilize (see page 11). If you make the quantity below, you will need (for example) two bottles, with a joint capacity of just over 1.5 litres/2¾ pints/6½ cups. They need not be the ones in which you plan to bottle your finished sloe gin.

1 Wash the sloes and dry them thoroughly.

2 Divide the sugar evenly among your sterilized bottles. If you are using a freshly emptied gin bottle, it will already be sterile. Now put on the radio or some good music and settle down with the pile of sloes and a big needle or a sharp skewer (Ginny favours a sweetcorn holder). Stab each sloe a few times and pop it into one of the bottles. Keep going until you finish the sloes. Pour the gin into the bottles; it should just cover the sloes. Secure the lids.

3 Put the bottles in a dark place (to protect the colour) and revisit them every day, turning them upside down. When all the sugar has dissolved, you can give them an occasional shake once in a while and, if you can bear it, leave them until December. By this point, the colour will have deepened through various shades of pink to a dark purple and the sloes will have shrivelled.

4 The sloe gin is now ready to be bottled. Select some pretty bottles and ensure they are thoroughly clean and sterile. Line a large sieve with muslin (cheesecloth) and strain the contents of both bottles through it into a large bowl or jug. Beware of lethally staining splashes! Using a funnel, pour the gin into the waiting bottles. It is ready to drink straight away, but can also be kept for several years: the colour will change from ruby to tawny and the flavour will become less plummy, more nutty.

Sloe gin is wonderful after a meal or poured over vanilla ice cream. And then there are cocktails…

Sloe Gin and Tonic
Mix one part ordinary gin with one part sloe gin. Top up with tonic water, a squeeze of lemon juice, a slice of lemon and some ice cubes.

Sloe Screw
Fill a large glass with ice. Pour in a measure of sloe gin and top up with orange juice. Stir well.

Sloe Gin Fizz
Pour a half measure of sloe gin into a champagne glass and fill with chilled dry sparkling wine.

Fruit with Pips

Crab apples, quinces and medlars are wonderful additions to your autumn kitchen. The fruits keep relatively well once picked and a good weighty haul can be achieved with very little effort. The greater difficulty is in finding the trees in the first place. Crab apples and very occasionally quinces can be found in hedges, although the apples you see on roadsides are often 'wildings', the fruit of discarded commercial apple cores, which don't grow true from seed. Medlars are harder to come by.

If you are lucky, you may know someone with an ancient kitchen garden or orchard where these trees would almost certainly have been cultivated. If not, we would seriously consider planting one or all of them in your own garden if you have space. None of the trees grows particularly tall and all are very pretty, especially when in blossom. If you plant two- or three-year-old saplings you will have a lovely array of fruit in a couple of years' time. Not only that but small children won't raid them, as they are all hard and taste pretty unpleasant raw, and even the birds won't look at them until there is nothing else left. This will give you plenty of time to pick what you need and stock up your pantry and freezer for the winter months ahead.

The image shows medlar fruit.

Crab Apples

If apples were the very first fruit, then crab apples were surely the very first apples. Until recently, it was believed that all orchard apples were the product of hybridization between crab apples and Asian apples. More recent research has questioned whether in fact the domestic apple arrived in Britain in pip form in the stomachs of horses from Asia, possibly before even the Romans got here. Whatever the outcome of that fascinating research into apple DNA, wild crab apples have been common in England, Wales and southern Scotland for thousands of years. They are usually found in ancient woods and in hedges and have small to medium-sized, yellowy green or red and extremely sour fruits, which ripen between August and October, depending on location and the weather.

Crab apples have only relatively recently been cultivated, but the range of cultivars is now vast. Their fruits range from the small, round, yellow Golden Hornet, barely bigger than a berry, to the enormous reddish-purple Wisley Crab, the size of a small Cox. John Downie, a medium-sized oval apple with yellow skin blushed with pink, is commonly held to be the best for jelly. To be honest we find any of the small to medium-sized fruits good (although juice yield from the smallest ones can be frustratingly low) and a blend is fine. Given the choice, we'd always favour the redder fruits because they make the most beautiful jelly, but the only ones to avoid entirely are the very large ones, which have a horrid dry texture, poor flavour and pathetic yield!

Crab Apple Jelly

2 kg/4½ lb crab apples, washed
  and roughly chopped
Approximately 900 g/2 lb/5 cups
  granulated sugar
Approximately 90 ml/3 fl oz
  lemon juice

*Makes about
8 large jars*

Jelly is absolutely the most wondrous thing to make with your basket of crab apples. Whether plain, flavoured with herbs (see page 139) or adorned with lavender (see below), a jar of jelly will make a fabulous gift, a delicious topping for your morning toast or will transform an ordinary roast into a feast. In fact, Caro's children won't contemplate roast chicken without it now! We also use the jelly, melted over a gentle heat, as a glaze for sweet fruit tarts.

1 The key thing when making jelly is not to be in a hurry! The first stage is the same whichever jelly you are planning to make with your juice, so it is quite sensible to cook and strain as many crab apples as possible and then freeze some of the juice for use at a later date. If you have a preserving pan you will be able to fit 4 kg/9 lb of apples in at once, so you can double up on the quantities above.

2 Simmer the crab apples in 1.2 litres/2 pints/5 cups water until the fruit is soft and mushy; this should take about 40 minutes. Tip the mixture into a jelly bag or a sieve lined with muslin (cheesecloth). Don't press the mixture through or your jelly will be cloudy, but just leave it to drip into a large bowl for at least 2 hours or, preferably, overnight.

3 Measure the juice and pour into a preserving pan or large saucepan. For every 600 ml/20 fl oz/2½ cups of juice, add 450 g/1 lb/ 2¼ cups sugar and 40 ml/scant 1½ fl oz/scant 3 tablespoons lemon juice. Place the pan over a low heat and stir gently until all of the sugar has dissolved. Increase the heat and boil rapidly, without stirring, until setting point is reached (see page 10). Remove from the heat and gently skim any scum from the surface, using a slotted spoon. Pour into warm, sterilized jars and seal immediately.

Lavender Jelly
Lavender jelly, spread thickly onto scones or crumpets, is a glorious teatime treat. Follow the Crab Apple Jelly recipe above. Once you have removed the scum, add 30 g/1 oz lavender petals to the jelly and stir in. You will need to wait for around 10 minutes before you pot the jelly so that it starts to thicken slightly. Stir gently now and then and when the petals remain distributed throughout the jelly rather than rising slowly, it is ready to be filled into warm, sterilized jars. Seal immediately.

It occurs to us that if you happened to have some lavender sugar instead of plain granulated, it would make the jelly even more perfumed and fabulous.

Herb Jellies

(mint, sage, thyme, rosemary, chilli)

These jellies are really delicious with roast meats (either on the side or stirred into the gravy) or in a cold meat sandwich and we even know of some chilli aficionados who eat their chilli jelly on toast for breakfast!

2 kg/4½ lb crab apples, washed
  and roughly chopped
Approximately 900 g/2 lb/5 cups
  granulated sugar
150 ml/5 fl oz/⅔ cup cider vinegar
Either 2 red chillies, quartered,
  seeds left in, or a medium bunch
  of mint, sage, thyme or rosemary
Either 2 tsp dried, crushed chillies
  or 4 tsp chopped mint, sage, thyme
  or rosemary leaves

Makes about 8 large jars

1 Follow the Crab Apple Jelly recipe on the previous page up to the stage where the juice has dripped through (the end of Step 2).

2 Measure the juice and pour into in a preserving pan or large saucepan. For every 600 ml/20 fl oz/2½ cups of juice, add 450 g/ 1 lb/2¼ cups granulated sugar and the vinegar. Depending on which jelly you are making, add either the quartered red chillies or the bunch of herbs and stir over a medium heat until the sugar has completely dissolved.

3 Increase the heat to high and boil without stirring until setting point is reached (see page 10). Remove from the heat and gently skim any scum from the surface, using a slotted spoon. Then remove the quartered chillies or bunch of herbs and replace with the crushed chillies or chopped herbs and stir thoroughly. Leave to cool slightly, stirring from time to time to redistribute the herbs or chillies; once they stop rising up through the jelly, pot into warm, sterilized jars and seal immediately.

Crab Apple Cordial

2 kg/4½ lb crab apples, washed
  and roughly chopped
Granulated sugar
Juice of 2–3 lemons

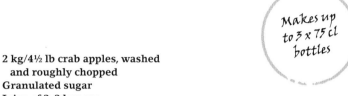

*Makes up
to 3 x 75 cl
bottles*

Cordials are a brilliant way to make a small amount of fruit stretch a long way. They will keep for up to 4 months if bottled following the method below; it's best to use smallish bottles because, once opened, fruit cordial must be kept in the fridge and drunk within a few days. It can also be frozen in plastic bottles or sterilized in a water bath (see page 11). It should be diluted to taste with water and can also be used diluted, 50:50, to make tasty and cost-effective ice lollies.

Crab apples are absolutely the best type of apples for making cordial, as not only do they produce a delightfully pink drink (assuming you are using red crab apples), but their intensely sour flavour and touch of bitterness means your cordial will have the strength of flavour and slight complexity to deliver a very thirst-quenching drink. The only potential problem is their high level of pectin – but that's easy to solve (see recipe right). The amount of juice produced by crab apples varies greatly, depending on the variety.

Each 500 ml/18 fl oz/2¼ cups of crab apple juice will produce about 1 litre/ 1¾ pints/4 cups of cordial.

1 Put the crab apples and 1.2 litre/2 pints/5 cups water in a large saucepan or preserving pan and bring slowly to the boil. Simmer gently until the apples are very soft and mushy. Tip the mixture into a jelly bag or a large sieve lined with muslin (cheesecloth) and leave overnight to drip into a large bowl. Do not press it through.

2 Measure the juice and return it to the cleaned pan. For every 500 ml/18 fl oz/2¼ cups of juice, add 350 g/12 oz/1¾ cups sugar, the juice of 2 lemons and an additional 250 ml/9 fl oz/generous 1 cup water. (This water is to dilute the pectin, to prevent the cordial from turning to jelly in the bottle.) Put the pan over a low heat and stir gently until the sugar has completely dissolved. Increase the heat and bring just to the boil, skim off any scum, then immediately pour into warm, sterilized bottles and seal.

Variations

Most fruits make lovely cordials, so feel free to experiment with any gluts you may have. Berries go particularly well with crab apples: try half and half crab apples and either wild raspberries or blackberries, but use only 700 ml/24 fl oz/scant 3 cups water.

Crab Apple Cheese & Butter

1.5 kg/3 lb 5 oz crab apples,
  washed and roughly chopped
Approximately 900 g/2 lb/5 cups
  granulated sugar
Glycerine (optional)

Makes about 6 large jars

No dairy involved! Cheeses and butters are traditional preserves made with the pulp of the fruit rather than straining off the juice. The main difference between the two is the level of set: butters are meant to be spread on bread or cakes (fantastic on toasted tea cakes!) and are really a smooth jam, whereas cheese is usually sliced and eaten with meat or cheese. We love crab apple cheese paired with roast pork or goose, as the tart flavour of the cheese cuts through the richness of the meat. The photograph shows Crab Apple Butter in the foreground, with Crab Apple Jelly (see page 133) behind.

1 Put the apples in a large saucepan or preserving pan and add just enough water to come about halfway up the apples. Cook over a low heat until the apples are soft and mushy. You can then either rub the contents of the pan through a sieve – arm-breaking work – or you can push it through a food mill on a fine setting, which will be infinitely easier. Weigh the pulp and return it to the cleaned-out pan. For every 600 g/1 lb 5 oz fruit, add 450 g/1 lb/2¼ cups sugar. Cook over a low heat, stirring frequently, until the sugar has completely dissolved. Increase the heat and boil rapidly, stirring to prevent the mixture from catching on the bottom of the pan.

2 If you are making butter, it is ready once it has thickened considerably and when you spoon some onto a plate no liquid oozes away from the dollop. Spoon into warm, sterilized jars and seal immediately.

3 Cheese takes a little longer – but not much, as crab apples are so full of pectin – and it will help if you have a clean plate in the freezer for testing the set. When you can briefly see the bottom of the pan as you scrape a wooden spoon across it, start testing. Put a spoonful of the mixture onto the cold plate; if it stays in a firm mound, it is ready. If not, keep cooking and test again after a few minutes.

4 Spoon into warm, sterilized jars and seal immediately. If you want to turn the cheeses out easily when you serve them, use straight-sided jars and brush a little glycerine inside each jar before filling.

Variation
Use 600 ml/20 fl oz/2½ cups cider to cover the apples and top up with water. Add ½ teaspoon each of ground cloves, cinnamon and nutmeg to the processed apple pulp for a lovely spiced preserve.

Pickled Crab Apples

Imagine how stunning these beauties will look on a plate with your Stilton, ham, duck or pheasant! They would also make a wonderful and unusual present, perfect for Christmas, as they should really be left to mature for a month or so.

Before you start, it is a good idea to pour the raw crab apples into jars to see how many they will make. Since the apples remain whole, it is hard to predict otherwise.

1 kg/2¼ lb/5 cups granulated sugar
600 ml/20 fl oz/2½ cups cider vinegar
2 strips of very thin lemon peel
4 cloves
4 black peppercorns
1 tsp crushed chilli flakes
1.5 kg/3 lb 5 oz similarly sized crab apples, washed and stalks removed

Makes approximately 4 x 500 ml/18 fl oz/ 2 cup Kilner-type jars

1 Put all of the ingredients except the crab apples into a large saucepan or preserving pan and heat gently, stirring from time to time, until the sugar has completely dissolved. Meanwhile, pack the crab apples into slightly cooled sterilized jars.

2 Boil the vinegar mixture vigorously for 5 minutes, then strain over the apples so that they are completely covered. Screw the lids on the jars immediately.

Variation
Replace the lemon, peppercorns and chilli with 1 tsp allspice berries and a 3–4 cm/1½ inch piece of fresh ginger, peeled and bruised.

Crab Apple Leather

1 kg/2¼ lb crab apples,
washed and roughly
chopped
Honey or granulated
sugar to taste

Makes 24 rolls of fruit leather

Drying is one of the most ancient methods of preserving fruit, dating back over 3000 years. Fruit leathers are intensely fruity and, compared with many 'fruity' snacks that you can buy, they are also incredibly wholesome. So you can feel very virtuous when you tuck a roll into your kids' lunchboxes.

We have to admit that we were initially sceptical, possibly finding the 'leather' word a little off-putting. However Caro's kids' reaction on first tasting them was emphatic and as they are easy and, dare we say it, foolproof to make, our resistance has melted! Fruit leathers have a myriad of uses: snip some over your muesli or porridge or add small pieces to fairy cakes in place of chocolate chips or raisins.

1 Preheat the oven to its lowest setting, no more than 100°C/210°F (not fan if possible, as the noise will drive you crazy after 12 hours or so!). Line two baking sheets (approximately 22 x 33 cm/8½ x 13 inches) with baking parchment or a non-stick liner.

2 Put the crab apples in a pan with 4 tablespoons water and cook gently until the apples are very soft and mushy. Push the mixture through a food mill on a fine setting; if you don't have a food mill you'll have to rub the mixture through a sieve – very hard work. Taste the purée and add honey or sugar to taste. If using sugar, you'll need to heat gently once the desired sweetness has been achieved, to dissolve the sugar.

3 Divide the mixture between the two baking sheets, smoothing evenly. Place in the oven and cook for approximately 12 hours, until the leather is completely dry, even at the centre. The first time you make the leather it is worth making them during a day when you can check on them every couple of hours or so because ovens can vary quite considerably. Once you know the right temperature setting, you should be able to cook up a batch overnight while you sleep.

4 Once cool, peel the leather off the parchment or non-stick liner and place onto a fresh piece of parchment, and then roll up the leather (and parchment) tightly. Store in an airtight container for up to 5 months and snip off coils as needed.

Variation
Replace half of the apples with 500 g/1 lb 2 oz blackberries, or experiment with other fruit such as damsons.

Crab Apple Sorbet with Bramble Coulis & Calvados Cream

Makes about 1 litre/1³⁄₄ pints/ 4 cups

Crab Apple Sorbet:
1 kg/2¼ lb crab apples, washed and roughly chopped
Approximately 140 g/5 oz/ scant ¾ cup granulated sugar
Juice of 1 lemon

Bramble Coulis:
250 g/9 oz blackberries
75 g/2¾ oz/⅓ cup granulated sugar
2 tbsp lemon juice

Calvados Cream:
300 ml/10 fl oz/1¼ cups double (heavy) cream
2–3 tbsp icing (confectioners') sugar
2–4 tbsp Calvados or other apple brandy

A fantastic way to combine the most evocative flavours of autumn in a blaze of glorious pink and purple. In France, where Caro spent her teenage years, the *trou normand*, an apple sorbet made with Calvados, is traditionally eaten during a large meal, just when appetites are flagging, to cleanse the palate and give the diners fortitude for the courses to come! For those of us made of less stern stuff, this recipe makes a light and refreshing pudding for when you have friends round for dinner.

If you make it with very pink crab apples, it comes out an amazing bubblegum colour, as in the photograph. You can make the sorbet and sauce well in advance, but the cream is best left till the last minute.

1 Put the crab apples in a pan with barely enough water to cover and cook gently until the apples are soft and mushy. Tip into a jelly bag or large sieve lined with muslin (cheesecloth) and leave for at least 2 hours or overnight to drip into a large bowl.

2 Measure the juice and return it to the cleaned pan with the lemon juice. For every 750 ml/25 fl oz/3 cups of crab apple juice, add 140 g/5 oz/scant ¾ cup sugar. Heat the mixture gently until the sugar has dissolved completely and then let it cool to room temperature.

3 Pour into an ice-cream maker and churn following the manufacturer's instructions. Alternatively, to freeze without an ice-cream maker, pour the mixture into a plastic container, cover and freeze, stirring briefly every 30 minutes or so to break up the ice crystals, until it has set (this will take 2–3 hours).

4 While the sorbet is freezing, make the coulis. Put all of the ingredients into a saucepan and heat until the fruit is soft and the sugar has dissolved. Then pass through a sieve or food mill on a fine setting and store it in the fridge.

5 Just before serving, make the Calvados cream: whip the cream until soft peaks form and whisk in the icing sugar and Calvados to taste.

6 The sorbet will keep in a covered container in the freezer for up to 2 months. The coulis will keep for 2–3 days in the fridge, or it can be frozen.

Quinces

Originally from central Asia, quinces have been used in Persian cooking for 2500 years and probably reached Britain in the thirteenth century, although there is some suggestion that the Romans may have cultivated them here. Quinces are known as the fruit of love, marriage and fertility and it is said that the golden apple Paris gave to Aphrodite was, in fact, a quince. Let's hope she didn't try and eat it. Beautifully golden they may be and with the headiest scent, but they are hard, sour and virtually inedible raw (even after you have washed off the down with which they are usually covered). See photograph on page 154.

The original marmalade was a Portuguese quince jam, *marmelada* (quince is *marmelo* in Portuguese), and quince paste exists in various forms across Europe: *pâte de coings* in France, *membrillo* in Spain, as well as our own quince cheese. However, the quince gradually fell out of favour in Britain, probably because it can't be eaten raw and is so difficult to peel and core.

It *is* worth persevering though, if you are lucky enough to lay your hands on some. Quinces add an incomparable fruity aroma and flavour to any dish and complement apples and pears wonderfully. They turn a beautiful reddish orange-colour when cooked and keep really well in a cool place.

Pickled Quinces

These magical slices of fragrant quince will enhance pretty much any cold meat or hard cheese and embellish your plate at the same time. Caro realized she might have changed her stance on pickled fruit (until then very much against) when she started fantasizing about how the deep orange quinces would be so beautifully accessorized by some pink peppercorns!

750 ml/1¼ pints/3 cups cider vinegar
400 g/14 oz/2 cups granulated sugar
4 tsp juniper berries
1 tsp pink peppercorns (or black if the pink are not available)
3 star anise
2 bay leaves
1.5 kg/3 lb 5 oz quinces, peeled, cored and halved

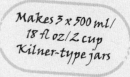

Makes 3 x 500 ml/ 18 fl oz/2 cup Kilner-type jars

1 Put all of the ingredients except the quinces into a large saucepan and bring to the boil, then simmer gently while you prepare the quinces. Slice each halved quince into four lengthways. Add them to the vinegar mixture and simmer gently until the quinces are just yielding to a sharp knife or skewer but are well short of fully soft. This will take only 3–4 minutes, so be vigilant.

2 Pack the quinces into warm, sterilized jars, share the spices among the jars and cover with the vinegar. Put the lids on and seal immediately.

3 As with most pickles, these will benefit from a couple of months undisturbed in their jars.

Quince Cheese

2 kg/4½ lb quinces, washed
  and cut into eighths
Juice of 6 lemons
Approximately 1.8 kg/4 lb/
  9 cups granulated sugar
Glycerine (optional)

Makes about 8 large jars

Richly autumnal quince cheese is the perfect partner for any mature, hard cheese such as cheddar and is also delicious with Stilton or sliced onto a pork chop prior to grilling it. We used to wonder how we would get through a whole batch of quince cheese. That's before we discovered the joys of adding a couple of spoonfuls to all manner of apple and pear puddings, as well as Moroccan stews. It's a little pot of magic! Now we almost have to start rationing it before the next crop appears in October.

1 Put the quinces in a large saucepan or preserving pan, add water to cover them, and simmer gently until the quinces are soft. This will probably take about 1 hour.

2 Now you need to reduce the quinces to a purée free of pips and skin. There's a hard way and a not-so-hard way. The hard way is to rub it through a sieve: this is seriously tough work. The not-so-hard way is to use a food mill on a fine setting – still quite tough, but bearable.

3 Weigh the quince purée and return it to the cleaned pan; add the lemon juice. For every 600 g/1¼ lb of purée, add 450 g/1 lb/2¼ cups sugar. Heat gently, stirring occasionally, until the sugar has completely dissolved. Put a plate in the freezer, for testing the set. Increase the heat to medium and cook the mixture until it has reduced, become thick and turned an orangey-red colour. You will need to stir continuously to prevent the mixture from catching and burning on the bottom of the pan, but be very careful because you are dealing with a culinary volcano, which will splutter red-hot fruit over you all the while. Make sure you have long sleeves and perhaps some glasses on. You will need to clean your kitchen floor afterwards, but it will all be worth it in the end.

4 When you can briefly see the bottom of the pan as you scrape a wooden spoon across it, start testing for set. Put a spoonful of the mixture onto the cold plate and leave it to cool. It should look distinctly orange compared with the original yellow and should quickly set into a firm mound with no juice oozing away. If not, keep cooking and test again after a few minutes.

5 Spoon into warm, sterilized jars and seal immediately. If you want to turn the cheeses out easily when you serve them, use straight-sided jars and brush a little glycerine inside each jar before filling.

Variation
If you prefer to make a sliceable cheese (as shown), cook for an additional 15 minutes until the mixture is very thick and dark. You can then set it in a shallow tin lined with parchment. It will keep in the fridge for a month.

Quince Jelly

This beautiful jelly is fabulous with pork, chicken or game, stirred into gravy, or as the ultimate indulgent topping for your morning toast. The fruit of love would make the perfect start to Valentine's Day.

2 kg/4½ lb quinces, washed
   and chopped
Approximately 900 g/2 lb/
   5 cups granulated sugar
Juice of 2 lemons
Glycerine (optional)

1 Put the quinces in a large saucepan or preserving pan, add water to cover them, and simmer gently until the quinces are very soft. This will probably take up to 1 hour, as they are so hard. Tip the mixture into a jelly bag or a sieve lined with muslin (cheesecloth). Don't press the mixture through or your jelly will be cloudy, but just leave it to drip into a large bowl for at least 2 hours or, preferably, overnight.

2 Measure the juice and return it to the cleaned pan; add the lemon juice. For every 600 ml/20 fl oz/2½ cups of juice, add 450 g/1 lb/ 2¼ cups sugar. Heat gently, stirring from time to time, until the sugar has dissolved. Increase the heat and boil rapidly, without stirring, until setting point is reached (see page 10). Pour into warm, sterilized jars and seal immediately.

Serves 6

Quince & Apple Sauce

A gorgeous twist on a traditional classic accompaniment for pork or roast goose.

2 medium-sized quinces, peeled,
   cored and roughly chopped (they
   should be about the same size as
   your apples)
Juice of ½ lemon
2 cooking apples, peeled, cored
   and roughly chopped
3 tbsp caster (superfine) sugar

1 Put the quinces in a saucepan with the lemon juice and 1 tablespoon water. Simmer gently until the quince is starting to soften. Add the apples and continue cooking for a few minutes.

2 Once the apples have started to go fluffy, add the sugar and cook, stirring gently, until the sugar has dissolved and the fruit is very soft. Mash with a fork or potato masher until reasonably smooth and serve with a flourish!

Lamb Tagine with Quinces

Most recipes for lamb tagine call for apricots or prunes, but quinces, with their wonderfully understated fruitiness, make an authentic and delicious alternative. When you have run out of fresh quinces, add a couple of tablespoons of quince cheese just before serving instead.

Tagine:
1.5 kg/3 lb 5 oz diced lamb
2 tbsp olive or vegetable oil
2 onions, sliced
2 garlic cloves, finely chopped
500 ml/18 fl oz/2 cups beef stock
400 g/14 oz canned chopped tomatoes
4 carrots, cut into matchsticks
1 tsp saffron threads
2 or 3 small quinces, peeled, sliced into eighths lengthways, core removed
Salt and pepper
150 g/5½ oz Kalamata or other black olives, pitted
Rind of 1 preserved lemon, rinsed and finely chopped

Marinade:
1 tbsp ground cumin
1 tbsp ground ginger
1 tbsp turmeric
1 tbsp paprika
1 tbsp ground cinnamon
2 garlic cloves, crushed
4 tbsp olive or vegetable oil

To Serve:
400 g/14 oz/2¼ cups couscous
400 ml/14 fl oz/1¾ cups boiling water
2 tbsp olive or vegetable oil
55 g/2 oz/6–7 tbsp pine nuts, toasted
Handful of fresh coriander (cilantro), chopped

1 Put all the marinade ingredients into a large bowl and mix thoroughly, add the lamb and stir well to coat. Place in the fridge to marinate for at least 2 hours.

2 Heat 2 tbsp oil in a large flameproof casserole dish over a medium heat and cook the lamb in batches until just browned, transferring each browned batch to a plate. Add the onions and garlic to the casserole and cook for a few minutes until the onion starts to soften. Return the meat to the casserole and add the stock, tomatoes, carrots, saffron and quinces and season to taste. Bring the mixture to the boil, then reduce the heat to very low, cover and simmer for 2 hours.

3 Add the olives and preserved lemon and continue to simmer gently, uncovered, for a further 30 minutes.

4 To serve, put the couscous in a large bowl and add the boiling water. Cover and leave to stand for 4 minutes. Stir in the oil and fluff up with a fork, then sprinkle in the pine nuts. Spoon into bowls and ladle the tagine on top. Garnish with a few coriander leaves.

Serves 4

Roasted Quinces

Quinces benefit from a relatively long, slow cooking; they also really need lemon and something sweet to bring out their full flavour. We have found roasting them an easy way to make a light and unusual pudding. If the skins are unblemished you can leave them on; you can also leave the cores for your guests to remove if you prefer. This will reduce the preparation time to almost nothing and is very easily done once the quinces are cooked.

**4 quinces, peeled, cored and cut into
    quarters lengthways
Grated zest and juice of 1 lemon
4 tbsp Marsala or other sweet wine
4 tbsp light muscovado sugar
4 tbsp caster (superfine) sugar**

1 Preheat the oven to 150°C/300°F/gas mark 2. Lay the quinces in an ovenproof dish, scatter over the remaining ingredients and cover with foil. Roast for about 2 hours, basting after 1 hour.

2 The quinces are ready when they are soft and have darkened edges; gently remove them to a serving dish. The liquid should be syrupy; if it is not, boil it in a saucepan for a few minutes before pouring it over the quinces.

3 Serve at room temperature, with crème fraîche or good vanilla ice cream.

Quince & Apple Tarte Tatin

Quinces will add an extra dimension to almost any apple or pear pudding; use quince cheese if you don't have any fresh fruit to hand. The only exceptions are puddings that include a light sponge or similar texture, as quinces are quite grainy and this just doesn't work when you are expecting a mouthful of yielding softness. Our only experiment involving sponge had to go in the bin – even the children wouldn't eat it!

If you don't have a tarte Tatin pan or ovenproof frying pan, prepare the fruit in an ordinary frying pan; when you remove the pan from the heat, immediately transfer the fruity mixture to a 22 cm/8½ inch diameter ceramic dish before covering with pastry.

Pastry:
140 g/5 oz/generous 1 cup plain (all-purpose) flour
pinch of salt
2 pinches of caster (superfine) sugar
115 g/4 oz/½ cup chilled butter, cubed
3–4 tbsp ice-cold water

Apple and Quince Topping:
55 g/2 oz/4 tbsp unsalted butter
150 g/5½ oz/¾ cup caster (superfine) sugar
800 g/1 lb 12 oz tart dessert apples, peeled, quartered and cored
1 large (or 2 medium) quince, peeled, cored and sliced into eighths (or quarters) lengthways

1 To make the pastry, put the flour, salt, sugar and butter into a food processor and blitz until reduced to crumbs. Put the crumbs in the freezer for about 30 minutes; if you do this, you won't need to rest the dough before rolling it out.

2 While the pastry crumbs are chilling, prepare the fruit. If the core is extremely difficult to remove, don't worry about keeping the slices of quince whole; it will be easier to remove the really hard parts of the core if you cut them in half widthways.

3 Put the butter into a tarte Tatin pan or cast-iron frying pan (skillet) with ovenproof handle, approximately 22 cm/8½ inch in diameter. Place over a low heat until the butter melts, then add the sugar. When the mixture starts to foam, add the apples and quince slices, arranging them in concentric circles with the quinces evenly distributed. Increase the heat to high until the juices turn a fudgey colour and the fruit has softened. Remove the pan from the heat and leave it to stand while you finish making the pastry.

4 Preheat the oven to 200°C/400°F/gas mark 6 and put a baking sheet into the oven. Return the pastry crumbs to the food processor and blitz while adding just enough ice-cold water for the dough to come together. This needs to be done as quickly as possible, but without adding so much water that the dough ends up wet.

5 Transfer the dough to a lightly floured surface and roll out thinly into a circle about 4 cm/1½ inches bigger than the tarte Tatin pan. Lift the dough over the pan and tuck down the sides under the apples, like tucking in a blanket. Transfer the pan to the baking sheet in the oven and cook for 20–30 minutes, until the pastry is beautifully browned and the appley syrup is bubbling.

6 Remove the tart from the oven and, using oven mitts, place a large serving plate face down over the tarte Tatin pan, then carefully but swiftly turn the whole arrangement the other way up. Lift off the tart pan and re-position any fruit that has become displaced. You should have a lovely mix of golden apples and orangey-pinkish quinces. Serve warm, with crème fraîche or good vanilla ice cream.

Medlars

Dog's bottom, cat's ditto – and that's before you let them go squishy almost to the point of rottenness in order to use them! No wonder this strange brown fruit has fallen out of such favour in our age of perfectly formed and colourful supermarket offerings.

The medlar has probably been cultivated for some 3000 years. It was popular in the Middle Ages and was traditionally eaten with port or wine after a meal; it was also highly regarded medicinally. An 18th-century recipe involves baking medlars in a shallow dish with butter and cloves and serving them like roasted apples.

The trees themselves are very attractive, with huge white blossoms and leaves that turn a gorgeous shade of red in autumn. The brown fruit is about the size of an apricot. It is fairly unprepossessing when picked, hard, from the tree in September to November, but the process of bletting, or leaving it to ripen, is necessary in northern climes, where it is not warm enough for the fruit to ripen on the tree. Shakespeare and others had many bawdy rhymes about the medlar, comparing it with fallen women since it becomes rotten almost as soon as it is ripe. In the Middle East, medlars are eaten straight from the tree, the flesh scooped out and topped with a little cream and sugar. That is not such an appealing prospect here when faced with a bletted fruit. The real reason to gather medlars is for the glittering prize of medlar jelly.

Medlar Jelly

Medlar jelly is the astonishingly beautiful, amber-coloured nectar that can be wrought from that ugly crop of mushy brown fruit sitting in a box in your garage. The flavour is complex and slightly smoky and goes sublimely well with game and poultry. It also tastes delicious with Stilton cheese.

Makes about 6 large jars

1.5 kg/3 lb 5 oz bletted medlars, washed and halved

3 lemons, washed and cut into eighths

Approximately 900 g/2 lb/ 5 cups granulated sugar

1 Put the medlars, lemons and 2 litres/3½ pints/8 cups water into a large saucepan or preserving pan and simmer until the medlars are mushy. Tip the contents of the pan into a jelly bag or a large sieve lined with muslin (cheesecloth) and leave to drip into a large bowl for several hours, preferably overnight. Do not squeeze, or your jelly will be cloudy.

2 Measure the juice and return it to the cleaned pan. For every 650 ml/22 fl oz/2¾ cups of juice, add 450 g/1 lb/2¼ cups sugar. Stir over a low heat until the sugar has completely dissolved. Then increase the heat and boil rapidly, without stirring, until setting point is reached (see page 10). This may take some time but don't panic, it should happen eventually. Pour into warm, sterilized jars and seal immediately.

Bletting medlars

The bletting process takes two weeks or more, depending on how cold it is. You should check your medlars frequently because there is a fine line between bletted and rotten. You don't have to follow the received wisdom of 80% bletted and 20% hard fruit as many recipes indicate: any combination of medlars that are wholly or partly soft will be fine. You will need to discard any that have desiccated, which will be obvious when you halve them and they are dry and crumbling.

Nuts

Nuts – wild or cultivated – have always been a highly prized food. They are generally high in protein, oil and carbohydrate, which makes them not only delicious but also a good source of energy for men and beasts alike. And here is the rub. We have a lot of competition to get our hands on wild nuts before some squirrel, bird or creepy crawly beats us to it! We need to stay alert and collect our share as soon as they are ready to drop, because there is nothing so special as a fresh, milky, squeaky new nut, eased from its casing.

The image shows a sweet chestnut.

Hazelnuts, Cobnuts & Filberts

Hazelnuts grow nearly everywhere in the British Isles and have been popular for millennia. An archaeological excavation of a site on Colonsay, off the west coast of Scotland, has recently turned up hundreds of thousands of toasted hazelnut shells from over 9000 years ago! Indeed, until recently they were seen as such an important foodstuff that before the First World War in many English villages, schoolchildren were given the day off on Holy Cross Day (14 September) to go nutting with their families.

You may see hazelnuts in other guises. Cobnuts and filberts are both cultivated forms of hazelnut grown in the UK. Kentish cobnuts were widely grown from the 1830s, and although the industry is much diminished from its heyday, it still exists and it is well worth purchasing some fresh cobnuts or cobnut oil, if you can.

It is tricky to pick wild hazelnuts at the right time. Too early, in August and early September, they will be soft and tasteless. They are ripe at just about the same time

as the leaves are turning yellow, in mid-September (see photograph page 165). You will probably need to pick them off the trees, as the ones on the ground tend to get infested and pillaged pretty quickly. Luckily, ripe nuts will keep fresh for a few months in a dry place, but after that it's best to roast them. However, they are so special we would recommend eating them all fresh and then buying dried ones when you run out.

When gathering hazelnuts, or buying them in their shells from a farmers' market, you will need about 500 g/1 lb 2 oz nuts in their shells to yield approximately 150–200 g/5–7 oz shelled nuts. If you then roast them, this reduces by a further 55 g/ 2 oz or so. Roasting the nuts really brings out the nutty flavour, and also makes it easy to rub off the skins. Spread them on a baking sheet and roast at 180°C/350°F/gas mark 4 for 5 minutes, but be vigilant, as it's easy to burn them. If the recipe calls for chopped roasted nuts, ideally you should you roast them up to a day in advance and leave them to cool before chopping.

Serves 4–6

Bircher-style Muesli with Fresh Hazelnuts

Dr Bircher-Benner invented this fruity/ fresh muesli for his hospital patients in Switzerland in the 1890s. Lucky patients! We think it is the most delicious breakfast, bar none. It is served in posh hotels, but it's also well worth making at home. It just needs a teeny bit of planning before you go to bed.

200 g/7 oz/2½ cups rolled porridge oats
400 ml/14 fl oz/scant 1¾ cups milk
150 g/5½ oz/generous ½ cup plain yogurt
40 g/1½ oz/4 tbsp raisins
40 g/1½ oz/4–5 tbsp pumpkin seeds
2 large crisp dessert apples (red-skinned ones look pretty)
Sugar or honey, to taste
40 g/1½ oz/1/3 cup fresh hazelnuts, chopped

1 Just before you go to bed, put the oats, milk, yogurt, raisins and pumpkin seeds in a bowl and mix together. Cover and chill overnight, during which time the muesli will become thicker because the raisins will plump up, the pumpkin seeds will soften a little and the oats will take up as much moisture as they possibly can. Don't be tempted to add the apples at this stage, or you will end up with unplumped oats and raisins, and lots of runny apple juice.

2 In the morning, quarter and core the apples, but do not peel them. Grate them coarsely and add the apples to the oat mixture. Sweeten to taste and spoon the muesli into bowls. Scatter the chopped hazelnuts over the top.

Fresh Hazelnut & Beetroot Salad

Serves 2

We love to use fresh green hazelnuts in salads. They add a special texture and a subtle, milky, sweet flavour.

Salad:
40 g/1½ oz/⅓ cup fresh
   hazelnuts
2 large beetroot, or a few smaller
   ones, cooked and peeled
2–3 little gem lettuces
1–2 sprigs of fresh thyme
100 g/3½ oz creamy goat's
   cheese
Salt and pepper

Dressing:
4 tsp cobnut (or hazelnut) oil
2 tsp sherry vinegar
2 tsp runny honey

1 Put all the dressing ingredients in a salad bowl and mix them together thoroughly.

2 Roughly chop the hazelnuts, leaving many good-sized pieces. Cut the beetroot into cubes or bite-sized pieces. Tear the lettuce leaves into the salad bowl and add the thyme leaves, stripped from the woody stems. Toss the leaves in the dressing until they are well coated. Throw the beetroot on top and scatter with pieces of goat's cheese. Finish by adding the hazelnuts, salt and freshly ground black pepper.

Apple & Hazelnut Stuffing

Serves 4–6

(for Roast Pork or Chicken)

Stuffing originated as a way both to eke out and to season precious meat. As with many humble foods, though, it has evolved, so that it can be a delicacy in its own right. We don't know why more people don't make their own stuffing. It's so easy, so totally different from the dried stuffing in a packet, and really, really delicious.

We are such fans that we never let old bread go to waste. When it is no longer a pleasure to eat fresh, we blitz the remnants of a loaf in the food processor and stick it in a bag in the freezer. Then when you want to make stuffing (or a crunchy topping for lasagne or a gratin, etc) it is simplicity itself to whip out the bag and crumble the frozen crumbs straight into the dish.

15 g/½ oz/1 tbsp butter, plus extra to finish
1 medium onion, finely chopped
1 celery stick, finely chopped
2–3 slices of bread (2–3 days old is best)
1 dessert apple, peeled, cored and chopped
50 g/1¾ oz/6 tbsp hazelnuts, roasted and roughly chopped
About 10–15 fresh sage leaves, shredded, or ½ tsp dried sage
Leaves from a large sprig of thyme, or ½ tsp dried thyme
Salt and pepper

1 Preheat the oven to 180°C/350°F/gas mark 4.

2 Heat the butter in a pan over a low heat, add the onion and celery and cook gently until very soft and translucent. Meanwhile, whizz up the bread, crusts and all, in a food processor to make reasonably fine crumbs.

3 Mix all the ingredients together in a large bowl and season with salt and pepper to taste. The mixture should not be wet, but should clump together as you mix it. If it doesn't, add a few drops of water. Press it lightly into an ovenproof dish, dot it with butter and cook it alongside your chicken, goose or pork for about 1 hour, or until crunchy.

4 Alternatively, you can stuff the neck end of the bird with the mixture and seal it up using cocktail sticks. The bird will look prettier, but you will miss out on the crunch. However, if you do this, remember to add the weight of the stuffing to that of the bird when you calculate cooking time.

Serves 8

Kentish Cobnut & Ginger Cake

This is an old-fashioned and quite sophisticated teatime treat. It is the polar opposite of a rich, showy cupcake. Its charm lies in its simplicity and subtlety: the crunch of roasted hazelnuts, moist chunks of apple and the warm, spicy sweetness of stem ginger. Luckily our kids don't like it, which is great, as we don't like sharing it!

225 g/8 oz/1¾ cups self-raising flour
1 tsp ground ginger
115 g/4 oz/½ cup butter, at room temperature, plus extra for greasing
115 g/4 oz/generous ½ cup soft light brown sugar
115 g/4 oz/scant 1 cup cobnuts (or hazelnuts), roasted, skinned and roughly chopped
4 pieces of preserved ginger in syrup, drained and roughly chopped
1 dessert apple, peeled, cored and chopped into smallish chunks
1 egg, beaten
125 ml/4 fl oz/½ cup milk
1 tbsp demerara sugar

1 Preheat the oven to 180°C/350°F/gas mark 4. Butter and line a 20 cm/8 inch diameter cake tin, ideally a springform or loose-bottomed tin.

2 In a large bowl, mix together the flour and ground ginger and rub in the butter until the mixture resembles fine breadcrumbs. Add the light brown sugar, 100 g/3½ oz/¾ cup of the chopped nuts, the chopped ginger and the apple. Mix it all together with the beaten egg and milk. Spoon the cake batter into the prepared tin. Scatter the remaining nuts on top and sprinkle with demerara sugar. Bake for about 45 minutes, or until a skewer inserted into the centre of the cake comes out cleanly. Leave to cool in the tin for 10 minutes, then transfer to a wire rack to cool completely.

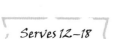

Serves 12–18

Hazelnut Choc Chip Cookies

These are American cookies, crisp on the outside, soft and chewy in the middle. They are at their very best while still warm from the oven, but we have found they are still delicious after a day or so, if a little chewier… If these cookies don't convince your children to like hazelnuts, then we're afraid probably nothing will!

115 g/4 oz/½ cup butter, at room temperature
100 g/3½ oz/½ cup caster (superfine) sugar
115 g/4 oz/generous ½ cup soft light brown sugar
1 egg
1 tsp vanilla extract
200 g/7 oz/generous 1½ cups plain (all-purpose) flour
½ tsp baking powder
85 g/3 oz chocolate chips or milk chocolate, chopped into chunks
85 g/3 oz hazelnuts, roasted and roughly chopped

1 Preheat the oven to 180°C/350°F/gas mark 4. Line a couple of baking sheets with baking parchment, or grease them with butter.

2 Using an electric mixer, cream together the butter and both sugars until really light and fluffy. Add the egg and vanilla and beat until well combined. Blend together the flour and baking powder, then fold the flour mixture, chocolate and hazelnuts into the butter mixture using a metal spoon.

3 Scoop the dough into rough balls and put them on the prepared baking sheets, spaced well apart, as they will spread during cooking. Bake for 10–12 minutes, until golden brown. Transfer to a wire rack and leave for a few minutes to firm up. Eat warm (ideally) or cold.

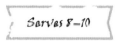

Raspberry & Filbert Torte

This is a bit of a riff on Linzer Torte, the Austrian classic, though it is easier to make and quite a bit lighter, since it dispenses with a lattice pastry topping in favour of some drizzled chocolate.

Hazelnut Pastry:
85 g/3 oz/⅔ cup filberts
   (or hazelnuts), roasted
85 g/3 oz/scant ¾ cup plain
   (all-purpose) flour
85 g/3 oz/6 tbsp butter
55 g/2 oz/¼ cup caster
   (superfine) sugar
grated zest of ½ lemon
1 egg yolk

Filling:
2–3 tbsp good-quality
   raspberry jam
400 g/14 oz fresh raspberries,
   ideally wild ones
100 g/3½ oz white chocolate

1 Preheat the oven to 180°C/350°F/gas mark 4. Butter a 24 cm/9½ inch diameter tart tin or dish.

2 Blitz the nuts in a food processor until they are finely and evenly ground. Add the flour, butter, sugar and lemon zest and pulse until they resemble fine breadcrumbs. (Or rub them in together by hand.) Add the egg yolk and 1 scant tablespoon water – you may only need half. Pulse again (or mix lightly) until the mixture comes together.

3 The dough will be very soft. Gather it into a ball and press it over the bottom and up the sides of the tart dish. If it sticks to your fingers, you may find it useful to put a spoon in some just-boiled water and use that to smooth the pastry out. Chill for 30–45 minutes. Then bake for about 20 minutes, until the pastry is evenly cooked and golden. Do not worry if the sides of the shell slump down a little. Leave it to cool.

4 For the filling, spread the raspberry jam over the bottom of the cooled hazelnut pastry and arrange the fresh raspberries on top. Finally, you need to melt the white chocolate, which is not always straightforward. You need to treat it gently and this is probably the time to make a 'double boiler'. Put a small saucepan with 2–3 cm/about 1 inch of water in the bottom on to simmer. Break the chocolate into chunks, and put them in a heatproof bowl that will sit on the top of the saucepan. The chocolate should melt slowly in the gentle heat. Using a spoon, drizzle the chocolate artfully over the raspberries, to make a web. Serve with whipped cream.

Cobnut Fudge

Ginny's grandmother was famous for her fudge. At Christmas, she would appear with a gigantic box, filled to the brim with differently flavoured, buttery, intensely sweet cubes. When we were kids, we couldn't understand why she bothered with anything other than vanilla. Nowadays, nutty ones are our favourites.

This is Granny's recipe. She didn't bother with weighing – it was 1 pack of butter, 1 bag of sugar and 1 large tin of evaporated milk. It makes an enormous amount! You could of course be sensible and scale it back. Out of nostalgia, we prefer to make the full quantity and think of some lucky person who deserves a present.

Note: The most important flavouring in this is the butter. It is simply not worth making with margarine.

250 g/9 oz/generous 1 cup good butter
1 kg/2¼ lb/5 cups granulated sugar
400 g/14 oz evaporated milk
250 g/9 oz/scant 2 cups cobnuts
   (or hazelnuts), roasted and chopped

Makes about 1.5 kg/3 lb 5 oz

1 You will need a baking sheet with a raised edge, about 18 x 33 cm/ 7 x 13 inches. Line it with baking parchment.

2 In a large, heavy-bottomed saucepan heat the butter, sugar and evaporated milk, stirring until the sugar has dissolved. Try to find a wooden spoon with a flat end, so you can properly scrape around the edges of the saucepan. Boil for about 10 minutes over a medium heat, to evaporate the milk further (imagine how long it would take if you started off with fresh milk!). Stir continuously, or it will burn on the bottom. In fact, it will probably burn at some stage anyway, unless you are incredibly diligent. If this happens, keep calm and carry on stirring. In the end the brown bits will mostly disappear and the nuts will disguise the rest.

3 You will start to notice the texture changing. Put a blob on a cold plate and study it. If, as it cools a bit, it looks/feels slightly granular, rather than smooth and toffeeish, it is ready. Leave to cool for about 5 minutes, then stir in 200 g/7 oz of the chopped nuts and stir thoroughly with a wooden spoon.

4 Pour the fudge into the prepared tin and scatter the remaining nuts on top. Gently flatten the surface to make sure the nuts will stick. When it is cool, though not completely cold, cut it into squares. with a very sharp knife.

Other flavours

Vanilla: add 1 tsp vanilla extract instead of the cobnuts
Walnut: use walnuts instead of the cobnuts
Orange: add the grated zest of 1 large orange instead of the cobnuts
Coffee: dissolve 1–2 tbsp instant coffee in about 2 tsp hot water – use as little water as you can – and add instead of the cobnuts
Chocolate: melt 200 g/7 oz dark chocolate (70% cocoa solids) and add instead of the cobnuts

Hazelnut Brittle

This is really easy and quick to make (not nearly as scary as it sounds) and makes a wonderfully more-ish present.

Makes approximately a 15 x 25 cm/ 6 x 10 inch rectangle

200 g/7 oz/1 cup granulated sugar
100 g/3½ oz/scant ¼ cup golden syrup
100 g/3½ oz/¾ cup hazelnuts, roasted and roughly chopped
55 g/2 oz/¼ cup butter
½ tsp vanilla extract
¾ tsp bicarbonate of soda (baking soda)

1 Place a sheet of baking parchment on a baking sheet.

2 Put the sugar and golden syrup into a saucepan and heat very gently, stirring continuously until all the sugar has dissolved. Then increase the heat and boil until the mixture reaches 110°C/230°F on a jam or sugar thermometer (or until it is bubbling furiously and starting to become more syrupy).

3 Add the hazelnuts to the pan and continue to boil until the syrup reaches 150°C/300°F or it suddenly turns darker and smells almost burnt. Remove from the heat immediately and stir in the butter, vanilla and bicarbonate of soda. Keep stirring vigorously until the butter has completely melted. Pour onto the parchment and leave to cool.

4 Once cold and hardened, the brittle breaks easily into pieces. Store in an airtight container for up to 10 days or wrap in cellophane and tie with ribbon for a delicious gift.

Chestnuts

Sweet chestnut trees are common in the south of England, though more unusual in Scotland, Wales and Ireland, and their nuts can be gathered from October to early November, when the kernels are fully brown, rather than white. They were introduced to the British Isles by the Romans, for whom they were an important food, and have long since become naturalized. Sweet chestnuts are not related to horse chestnuts, though the nuts have a passing resemblance. Do not feel tempted to try a conker: although they are easier to get at because their cases are nowhere near as prickly, the nuts are toxic and not even vaguely delicious.

Sweet chestnuts, on the other hand, are very good to eat in both sweet and savoury dishes – and should not just be for Christmas. For a nut, they are surprisingly low in fat (3%) and high in carbohydrates. and in parts of continental Europe, chestnut flour used to be a staple food, dried and ground into flour for use throughout year.

Getting the nuts out of their extremely prickly green casings, which bear more than a passing resemblance to a sea urchin, is just the first step on the road to eating your chestnuts. The traditional method is to stamp on the casings and hope they contain a nut or two of a reasonable size. Really, do not bother with small nuts. There are still a few time-consuming steps to go and the effort:reward ratio is unbelievably poor for the small ones. This is because, unlike other nuts, chestnuts need to be cooked before you can eat them.

Alternatively, if you are going to cook any of the recipes below, an easier way to get at the nuts is to boil them. Cut a cross in the leathery shell first and boil them for at least 10 minutes. Pull them out of the water one at a time and, using rubber gloves, peel away the outer shell and the inner, bitter skin. This is a bit of a labour of love, so if you are short of time, you may opt to buy a box of vacuum-packed chestnuts from the supermarket (shhhhh!). On the other hand, if you manage to produce more chestnuts than you need, they can be very successfully frozen. Weigh and label the peeled chestnuts before freezing so they are ready to use. As a very rough guide, if you pick 500 g/1 lb 2 oz chestnuts – that's the weight after you've removed the green casings – you should end up with beween 250 g/9 oz and 350 g/ 12 oz of peeled nuts.

Chestnut & Chorizo Soup

(Sopa de Castañas)

This recipe is adapted from Sam and Sam Clark's *Moro* cookbook. It's a real Spanish classic and although it's not a looker, it can't be beaten in taste terms. The sweetness of the chestnuts offset the salty, spicy chorizo to great effect, and the colour of the soup matches the rich autumnal colours outside.

4 tbsp olive oil
1 large Spanish onion, diced
1 medium carrot, diced
1 celery stick, thinly sliced
150 g/5½ oz mild cooking chorizo, cut into 1 cm/½ in cubes
Salt
2 garlic cloves, thinly sliced

1 tsp ground cumin
1½ tsp fresh thyme leaves
1–1½ tsp dried crushed chilli
200 g/7 oz cherry tomatoes, roughly chopped
500 g/1 lb 2 oz peeled chestnuts, roughly chopped
20 saffron threads, infused in 3–4 tbsp boiling water

1 In a large saucepan, heat the olive oil over a medium heat. Add the onion, carrot, celery, chorizo and a pinch of salt and cook for about 20 minutes, stirring occasionally, until everything caramelizes and turns quite brown. This gives the soup a wonderful rich colour and flavour.

2 Now add the garlic, cumin, thyme and chilli and cook for 1 minute. Add the tomatoes and cook for about 2 minutes, then add the chestnuts. Give everything a good stir, then add the saffron-infused liquid, and 1.1 litre/just over 1¾ pints/4½ cups water, and simmer for about 10 minutes.

3 Remove from the heat and mash, using a potato masher, until almost smooth but still with a little bit of texture. Season with salt to taste and serve.

Roasting chestnuts

Once home, you can slit the skin of each chestnut and roast them over an open fire in a chestnut pan (or an empty tin can held with tongs). Slitting the skin is essential, otherwise the chestnuts will explode. This is the traditional way to eat them and it is exceptionally good. In our experience, the inviting smell means it's hard to wait until they are properly cool before trying to peel them open. Burned, charry fingers are the inevitable result, but it seems to be all part of the fun.

Christmas Chestnut & Sausagemeat Stuffing

It is incredibly satisfying to serve something lovely on Christmas Day that you have gathered or grown yourself, so we *try* to freeze some shelled chestnuts and save them for Christmas. This is a family recipe, perfected and refined over the years, and for us it is the essence of Christmas. It goes equally well with turkey, goose or even chicken – and can be stuffed into the bird or cooked separately in a loaf tin. We always make lots, so it can be sliced with the cold meats and salads on Boxing Day.

2 tbsp olive oil
2 large onions, finely chopped
4 large celery sticks, finely chopped
400 g/14 oz peeled chestnuts,
  roughly chopped
85 g/3 oz dried cranberries
500 g/1 lb 2 oz good sausagemeat
Grated zest of 1 large lemon
1 heaped tsp dried thyme
Big handful of fresh parsley,
  chopped
1 egg

Enough for 12 without leftovers, or 6 with

1 Heat the oil in a pan over a low heat and sweat the onions in the oil until they are sweet and translucent. Leave them to cool.

2 In a large bowl, combine all the ingredients thoroughly. You will probably need to use your hands and squish them together. Loosely stuff the mixture into the neck end of the bird. Remember to leave enough room for it to expand or it will find a way to escape during cooking. Secure the skin with cocktail sticks. Remember to add the weight of the stuffing to that of the bird when you calculate cooking time.

3 If there is more stuffing than will fit in the bird (which is almost inevitable), butter an ovenproof dish and fill it with the remaining stuffing. Roast it alongside the other things you are cooking at about 180°C/350°F/gas mark 4 for 45 minutes–1 hour, until it is cooked through. Keep an eye on it and it it appears to be browning too much, cover it with foil.

Happy Christmas!

Serves 4

Beef, Beer & Chestnut Suetcrust Pie

This is a wonderfully rich and warming dish. Perfect with a good bottle of red and a favourite DVD. If you prefer, the suetcrust can be replaced by puff pastry, or even shortcrust. However, if you haven't tried suetcrust recently, we would urge you to have a go. It's incredibly easy to make and it adds to the beefiness of this pie.

Ideally, make the casserole filling the day ahead. Keeping it for a day will allow the flavours to develop and if it's already cool, it is much easier to deal with the pastry lid.

Filling:
2 tbsp vegetable or olive oil
200 g/7 oz streaky bacon or
    pancetta, cubed
12 small shallots, peeled
500 g/1 lb 2 oz braising steak, cubed
2 tbsp plain (all-purpose) flour
330 ml/11 fl oz/1 ⅓ cups bitter
    or stout
125 ml/4 fl oz/½ cup beef stock
1 tbsp crab apple or redcurrant jelly
200 g/7 oz peeled chestnuts
250 g/9 oz chestnut (cremini)
    mushrooms, halved
1 bay leaf
1 sprig of thyme
Salt and pepper

Suetcrust Pastry:
175 g/6 oz/1½ cups self-raising
    flour, plus extra for dusting
Pinch of salt
85 g/3 oz shredded suet
1 tbsp milk, to glaze
Salt crystals (optional)

1 Preheat the oven to 150°C/300°F/gas mark 2.

2 Pour a little of the oil into a pan over a low heat, add the bacon cubes and cook until the fat has largely run out of them. Remove them with a slotted spoon and place in a flameproof casserole dish. Add the shallots and cook in the bacon fat until golden brown, then remove them and add to the bacon. Toss the braising steak in the flour and cook the meat in the same pan for 4–5 minutes, until browned all over. Put the meat into the casserole and deglaze the pan with the beer.

3 Tip the beer and meat juices into the casserole and add the stock, jelly, chestnuts, mushrooms, bay leaf and thyme. Bring just to the boil, season with salt and pepper, then put the dish into the oven and cook for 2–2 ½ hours, or until the meat is tender. Taste and adjust the seasoning and leave to cool, overnight if possible.

4 Preheat the oven to 180°C/350°F/gas mark 4.

5 Find a pie dish large enough to hold the meat comfortably (we used a 24 x 17 cm/9½ x 6½ inch enamel pie dish with a wide rim). Pour the beef casserole into the dish.

6 To make the pastry, put the flour and salt into a mixing bowl and stir in the suet. Add 5–6 tbsp cold water and mix to form a dough. Using your hands, bring it together into a ball. Sprinkle some flour onto a work surface and over the dough, then roll out the dough in the shape of your pie dish. Dampen the rim of the dish with water and place the dough on top. Press it firmly onto the rim, to ensure it's sealed. Brush some milk over the pastry and cut a few slits in it to allow steam to escape. If you like, scatter some salt crystals over the pastry. Bake for 30–35 minutes, until golden. Serve with wilted spinach or steamed savoy cabbage.

Chestnut Preserve with Vanilla & Rum

Makes about 2 large jars

500 g/1 lb 2 oz chestnuts, all outer skins and membranes removed (you'll need to gather just over 1 kg/2¼ lb of chestnuts)
250 g/9 oz/1¼ cups granulated sugar
1 vanilla pod
About 150 ml/5 fl oz/⅔ cup rum

This preserve hails from France, where chestnuts are yet another of those wild things that seem to be more appreciated there than in the UK. Caro spent her teenage years in southern France – crème de marrons was often on the school lunch menu and was absolutely wolfed down by all the children. This is a grown-up version, flavoured with rum.

You wouldn't want to spread this preserve on toast at breakfast, but it will help you make 1001 luscious desserts. It can be blended into whipped cream, buttercream or chocolate ganache to become a decadent icing or filling for cakes, roulades or crêpes, or it can be mixed with cream and spooned or piped into delicate pastry shells and topped with grated chocolate and Chantilly cream.

1 Firstly, you have to peel those chestnuts! (See page 172.) After you have removed the outer shell, boil them again, for about 45 minutes, until they are really soft. Make sure you get rid of all the horrible membranes and any bits of hard or rotten nut. Blitz the nuts in a food processor until quite finely ground. Now you can relax, as it's much easier from here on in.

2 Put the sugar in a heavy-bottomed pan and add 200 ml/7 fl oz/generous ¾ cup water. Roll the vanilla pod between your fingers to soften it, then open it up and scrape out the seeds with a knife. Add the seeds and pod to the pan and place over a low heat until all the sugar has dissolved.

3 Add the ground chestnuts and simmer the mixture for about 20 minutes, stirring more or less continuously, to prevent it from catching on the bottom. It will be quite thick and dry. Add the rum and simmer gently for 10 minutes: the alcohol will evaporate, leaving behind the rum flavour. Remove the vanilla pod and ladle the preserve into warm, sterilized jars (see page 10).

Chocolate & Chestnut Terrine

400 ml/14 fl oz/scant 1¾ cups whipping or double (heavy) cream
150 g/5½ oz dark chocolate (70% cocoa solids),
broken into chunks, plus extra to decorate
300 g/10½ oz chestnut preserve with vanilla and rum (see above)

This is one of our favourite ways of using chestnut preserve. It is a quick and easy posh dinner party dessert and can be made in just 5 minutes, plus you need to allow chilling time (see recipe).

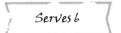

Serves 6

1 Line a 450 g/1 lb loaf tin with clingfilm (plastic wrap).

2 Whip 325ml/11 fl oz/scant 1½ cups of the cream until it forms soft peaks. Keep the remaining cream in the fridge. Melt the chocolate, either in the microwave or in a bowl over a pan of simmering water. Mix it into the chestnut preserve and then fold the mixture into the cream. Pile everything into the lined loaf tin and put it into the fridge for 6 hours, or the freezer for 1 hour.

3 To serve, turn out the terrine onto a pretty plate. Whip the remaining cream and spread it over the top. Sprinkle generously with grated chocolate. Slice it into neat portions and serve with extra pouring cream, if liked.

Walnuts

Walnut trees originate in southern Europe, though they have been grown in gardens and parks in the British Isles for at least 500 years and many have escaped, the seeds spirited away by animals. However, walnuts have never been a commercial crop in this country, so we have included them in our loose interpretation of 'wild food'.

Come October, if you are not lucky enough to have a source of fresh, wet walnuts, all is not lost because they can sometimes be found in greengrocers and farmers' markets. If you are taking them directly from the tree, remember that the nut is encased in a green, leathery, inedible husk. Removing this will reveal the hard,

wrinkly walnut shell, which in turn encloses the nut or, technically, the seed. Once picked, walnuts should be kept in their shells in a cool, dry place to maximize their useful lives. The yield is not high – 500 g/1 lb 2 oz walnuts in their shells will give you about 200–250 g/ 7–9 oz of edible nut – but the flavour of fresh walnuts is incomparable.

Lately, walnuts have gained something of a superfood reputation. It appears that they are not only very nutritious, being high in oil and protein, but the oils and antioxidants they contain may actually be extremely good for us and limit some of the damage done to our systems by saturated fats.

Pickled Walnuts

2 kg/4½ lb green walnut drupes
450 g/1 lb salt
1 litre/1¾ pints/4 cups cider
  vinegar
500 g/1 lb 2 oz/2½ cups dark
  brown sugar

2 tbsp whole peppercorns
1 tbsp allspice berries
9 cloves
3 blades of mace
3 tbsp grated fresh root ginger

A curiously English delicacy, this one has never travelled to continental Europe. The fact it is made with immature, unripe nuts or 'drupes', including the green husk, before the shell has hardened, may be the clue. In some years, British walnuts just don't ripen satisfactorily, so it may have been a good idea to take some early and pickle them. At least you had something to show for your tree!

Anyhow, whatever the reason for their invention, pickled walnuts are a fine thing to have with strong cheeses and cold meats. Sliced thinly, they can make a fantastic sweet/sour contribution to a fishy salad; roughly chopped, they add piquancy to a beef stew. Unopened, they will keep for years; once opened, store in the fridge for up to 4 weeks.

The key thing is to harvest your nuts/drupes early enough. They should be just about perfect around mid-June, but you need to check each one by pushing a needle into it, to ensure the hard shell has not yet formed. (The other key thing to know is that you must never, ever handle one of these green walnuts without your trusty rubber gloves on. Walnut juice is an extremely powerful brown dye!)

1 Using rubber gloves, pierce each drupe a few times with the tines of a fork (stainless steel or silver, not iron, as this will taint). Place the walnuts in a clean bucket and add enough water to cover them. Add 225 g/8 oz of the salt and stir. Leave to soak for a week. Drain and repeat the process with fresh brine for a second week.

2 Drain the walnuts and lay them out to dry on trays. After about 3 days they will have turned black, which means they are ready to pickle. It is safest to redo the needle test at this point and discard any walnuts that seem firm to hard.

3 Put the vinegar and the sugar into a large, heavy-bottomed pan. Put all the spices into a piece of muslin (cheesecloth) and tie up the ends with string. Add this to the pan and bring the mixture to the boil, stirring occasionally. Meanwhile, rinse the walnuts. When the vinegar is boiling, add the walnuts, bring back to the boil and then simmer for 15 minutes. Remove from the heat and remove the spice bag.

4 Spoon the walnuts into the warm, sterilized jars (see page 10) and top up with the sweet vinegar, to within 1 cm/½ inch of the top of the jar. Seal and store in a cool place for about 3 months before opening.

*Makes 5 or 6
500 ml/18 fl oz/2 cup
Kilner-type jars*

Roquefort & Pear Salad with Walnuts

Serves 2 for lunch or 4 as a starter

This is probably our favourite salad of all time. We often make it for lunch when we are working together. The salty, acidic tang of the cheese, sweet juiciness of the pear and bittersweet crunch of the walnuts makes it a sensory feast, which we find both satisfying and energizing. It also makes a good starter.

Salad:
4 heads of white chicory, sliced
1–2 pears, cored and thinly sliced or cut into small dice
55 g/2 oz Roquefort cheese, cut into smallish cubes
55 g/2 oz/½ cup walnuts, roughly chopped
Freshly ground black pepper

Dressing:
2 tsp Dijon mustard
Juice of ½ lemon
Dash of cider vinegar
1 tsp runny honey (optional)
About 4 tbsp olive or rapeseed (canola) oil
Salt

1 First, make the dressing. Put all the ingredients into a small jar and shake vigorously. Taste and adjust the seasoning.

2 To make the salad, mix together the chicory and pears in a salad bowl. Add the dressing and toss until they are well coated. Scatter the cheese and walnuts on top and finish with a generous grinding of aromatic black pepper. Serve with good bread.

Mushrooms Stuffed with Stilton & Walnuts

Serves 4

A starter or light lunch, which looks glamorous, tastes delicious, but takes practically no effort to produce (not counting shelling the walnuts!). Portobello mushrooms sometimes look unfeasibly enormous, but they really do shrink in the oven. You can also make these as hot canapés, using small mushrooms topped with a walnut half.

8 large portobello mushrooms
225 g/8 oz Stilton cheese, crumbled
Generous handful of parsley, finely chopped
115 g/4 oz/1 cup walnuts, chopped

1 Preheat the oven to 180°C/350°F/gas mark 4. Generously butter a large baking sheet.

2 Pull the stalks out of the mushrooms and place the mushrooms, gills up, on the baking sheet. Put them in the oven for 10 minutes.

3 Remove the baking sheet from the oven and crumble the Stilton into the mushroom cavities, sprinkle over some parsley and top with the walnuts. Bake for about 15 minutes, until the cheese is bubbling and the nuts are toasted. Serve hot, with salad leaves.

Walnut Soda Bread

200 g/7 oz/2 cups walnuts
450 g/1 lb/scant 4 cups
   wholemeal (whole wheat) flour
1 tbsp demerara sugar
2 tsp bicarbonate of soda (baking
   soda)
1 tsp salt
500 g/1 lb 2 oz/2 cups plain
   yogurt – low-fat is fine

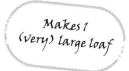

*Makes 1
(very) large loaf*

We became passionate about freshly baked soda bread after being introduced to it by a lovely lady called Caroline Tod. Her bread has a moist, nutty wheatiness with a dense, sweet crumb and crunchy crust and it is really, really yummy. It has bags more flavour than normal bread and goes perfectly with cheese, soup, marmalade...we could go on. Plus, it is incredibly easy to make and seems to keep for a week without becoming stale or dry. She has very kindly given us her recipe.

1 Preheat the oven to 180°C/350°F/gas mark 4 and either lightly oil a baking sheet (for a freeform, traditional loaf) or oil a 900 g/2 lb loaf tin – or use a loaf tin liner – for a conventional loaf shape.

2 Divide the walnuts into two roughly equal amounts. Blitz one half in a food processor until you have a coarse powder. Chop the rest into largish chunks. Put all the walnuts into a large bowl and add the remaining dry ingredients; mix well to ensure the bicarbonate of soda is evenly dispersed.

3 Stir in the yogurt and mix to a soft dough. Bring it all together with your hands, but do not knead it. This bread benefits from being handled as little as possible. Turn it out onto a well-floured surface. If you are going to bake it in a loaf tin, form the bread into a log shape and drop it into the tin. If not, form it into a ball, place it on the oiled baking sheet and score a deep cross into the top, using a sharp knife.

4 Bake for about 50 minutes, until well risen and browned. Leave to cool on a wire rack for about 30 minutes before tucking in.

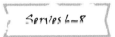
Serves 6–8

Lemon & Walnut Meringue Cake

Meringue:
4 egg whites
250 g/9 oz/1¼ cups caster (superfine) sugar
150 g/5½ oz/1½ cups walnuts, chopped
300 ml/10 fl oz/1¼ cups double (heavy) cream
3–4 tbsp good-quality lemon curd (homemade is best)

Lemon Curd:
4 egg yolks and 2 eggs, beaten
200 g/7 oz/1 cup caster (superfine) sugar
100 g/3½ oz unsalted butter
Grated zest and juice of 4 unwaxed lemons
Makes 2 standard jars

When we were children our mums never supplied the kind of puddings we really yearned for. Caro's mum didn't have a sweet tooth at all and had a policy of keeping the fridge stocked with yogurts for those that did. Ginny's mum made classic British puddings, such as wonderful crumbles and lemon meringue pies, but never really went for what you could call, in true 1970s' style, a 'gateau'. Luckily, some of our friends had mothers who were more obliging.

This is Liz Semple's recipe and it has survived on a battered piece of card in Ginny's 12-year-old handwriting because it is simply delicious: sweet, nutty, citrussy-sour and gooey. And it's also a complete doddle to make. It is quite a wonder how the walnuts totally transform the texture and taste of the meringue.

1 Preheat the oven to 180°C/350°F/gas mark 4. Cut two squares of baking parchment to fit on two baking sheets.

2 Whisk the egg whites with an electric mixer until soft peaks form. Add half the sugar and whisk in, then add the remaining sugar and whisk until very stiff. Fold in most of the chopped walnuts, reserving some for decoration.

3 Divide the mixture in half and spread each half into a circle about 20 cm/8 inches in diameter, on one of the pieces of baking parchment. The meringue should be 2–3 cm/about 1 inch thick. It will expand in the oven, so don't go too close to the edge of the paper. Bake for about 40 minutes; after about 30 minutes check that the meringues are not burning. Leave to cool.

4 To make the lemon curd, place all of the ingredients into a bowl set over a pan of simmering water. Whisk gently until the sugar has dissolved and then continue to cook gently, whisking frequently, until the mixture has thickened enough to coat the back of a spoon. Pour immediately into warm, sterilized jars and leave to cool. Store in the fridge and use within 2 weeks.

5 Just before serving, whip the cream until it holds its shape and mix in the lemon curd to taste. Put the largest meringue on a serving plate and spread it with half the lemon cream. Carefully place the other meringue on top and spread with the remaining cream. Finish with a sprinkling of chopped walnuts.

Walnut & Brandy Truffle Cake with Blackberry Sauce

Truffle Cake:
100 g/3½ oz/1 cup walnuts
70 g/2½ oz/⅓ cup caster (superfine) sugar
15 g/½ oz/2 tbsp unsweetened cocoa powder
125 g/4½ oz/½ cup plain yogurt – use goat's or sheep's milk yogurt if you prefer
2 eggs
1 tsp vanilla extract
100 ml/3½ fl oz/7 tbsp brandy
150 g/5½ oz dark chocolate (70% cocoa solids), broken into chunks

Blackberry Sauce:
300 g/10½ oz blackberries, fresh or frozen
100 g/3½ oz/½ cup granulated sugar

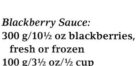
Serves 6

This is a pretty dense, sophisticated, adult cake, to cut in thin slices and savour with coffee. The blackberry sauce is an optional extra, but we find the sharp earthiness of the fruit cuts the chocolate in a very lovely way. If you haven't got blackberries, raspberries would also be good.

What might be less obvious about this cake is that it is relatively virtuous, containing no flour and little fat (except for that contained in the nuts, yogurt and chocolate). We are always excited to find recipes like this because we have a very good friend who is wheat- and dairy-intolerant – and we hate for her not to be able to join us for pudding. Many people who are dairy-intolerant are sensitive to cow's milk products but find they can eat sheep's and goat's milk. In case you're wondering, good-quality dark chocolate contains no dairy ingredients.

1 Preheat the oven to 150°C/300°F/gas mark 2. Lightly oil and line the bottom and sides of a 17 cm/6½ inch round cake tin, ideally a springform or loose-bottomed tin.

2 Put the walnuts, sugar and cocoa in a food processor and pulse until the walnuts are evenly ground. Add the yogurt, eggs, vanilla and brandy and pulse briefly.

3 Melt the chocolate in a heatproof bowl, either over a pan of simmering water or in the microwave, giving it 30-second blasts until the chocolate has melted. Add the chocolate to the walnut mixture and pulse a couple of times until it is fully blended.

4 Pour the batter into the prepared tin and bake for about 60 minutes, until it has risen evenly, but retains a slight wobble. Leave it in the tin to cool completely. Be prepared: this cake will probably sink.

5 While it is cooling, make the sauce. Put the blackberries and sugar in a saucepan, add 100 ml/3½ fl oz water and bring to the boil. Simmer for a couple of minutes, until the blackberries are soft. Whizz them with a handheld blender and push through a sieve to get rid of the seeds. Leave to cool.

6 Dust the cake with icing (confectioners') sugar and serve with a jug of the sauce.

Index

Authors' acknowledgements

We would like to thank our mothers Roo and Jenifer who, in their idiosyncratic ways, launched us on a lifetime's enjoyment of the countryside and of cooking as well as Jim and Mark who have gone above and beyond husbandly duties to help us and tolerated Wild at Heart's invasion into their lives and homes.

We are indebted to all those who have helped us to launch Wild at Heart, especially Mary and Clive Edmed and Richard Greenwood who have been stalwart and generous supporters.

Thanks, too, to our kind friend Peter Stanford and to all those at Anova who worked on the book, especially Fiona Holman, Georgie Hewitt, Allan Somerville and Maggie Ramsay. Finally, thanks to Cristian Barnett for his patient humour and fabulous photos.

Picture acknowledgements